Peter Hudson

is thirty. He was educated at Winchester College and has spent the years since then travelling in Canada, the USA, Europe and Cuba, but principally in Africa. His first journeys there, in 1982, took him to Botswana, Zimbabwe, Zambia, Malawi, Tanzania and Kenya. In 1985, he spent a year travelling through the continent visiting Morocco, Algeria, Mali, Guinea, Liberia, the Ivory Coast, Burkina Faso, Niger, Chad, Cameroon, the Central African Republic, Zaire, Uganda, Kenya, Somalia, Djibouti and Egypt. Some of this trip was described in his first book, *A Leaf in the Wind*, which was shortlisted for the 1988 Thomas Cook Travel Book Award. Peter Hudson's next visit to Africa in 1988 took him to the Gambia, Senegal, Mauritania and back to Mali. *Travels in Mauritania* records some of his experiences during that trip.

Also by Peter Hudson

A LEAF IN THE WIND

PETER HUDSON

Travels in Mauritania

Flamingo
An Imprint of HarperCollins*Publishers*

Flamingo
An imprint of HarperCollins *Publishers*,
77–85 Fulham Palace Road,
Hammersmith, London W6 8JB

Published by Flamingo 1991
9 8 7 6 5 4 3 2 1

First published in Great Britain by
Virgin Books
1990

ISBN 0 00 654358 8

Set in Plantin

Printed in Great Britain by
HarperCollins Manufacturing Glasgow

For Marie

Contents

Part Three: Journeys in Mauritania, the nation

Acknowledgements

I should like to thank the people of the Islamic Republic of Mauritania for allowing me to wander so freely and so safely about their country, and for unfailingly giving me the best of traditional desert hospitality wherever I went. For reasons of security, the names of some people mentioned in my book have been changed but I should like to offer them, and all those many people whose names one never gets to know, a particularly warm 'thank you' for going out of their way to befriend a solitary traveller.

I should also like to thank Isla Maclean for all the help and encouragement she has given me in my dealings with Mauritania; Hugo and Nonni Meynell for very kindly providing a peaceful room for me to write in; Vikki Tate for her typing; my sister Veronica Hudson for her drawings; Caroline Erskine for her work on my photographs; Serafina Clarke for being my agent; Gill Gibbins for being my hard-working editor; and my parents for being there.

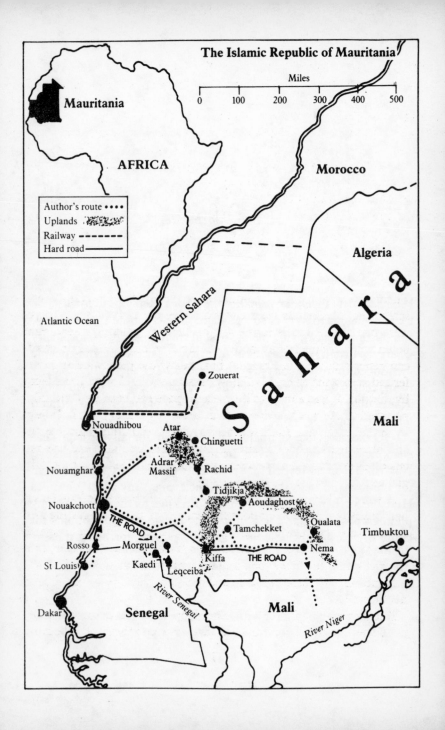

The Islamic Republic of Mauritania

Miles

0   100   200   300   400   500

Mauritania

AFRICA

Morocco

Algeria

Author's route ••••
Uplands
Railway -------
Hard road ———

Western Sahara

Atlantic Ocean

Sahara

Mali

Zouerat

Nouadhibou

Atar   Chinguetti

Nouamghar   Adrar   Rachid
                 Massif

Nouakchott   Tidjikja
                         Aoudaghost
        THE ROAD   Oualata   Timbuktou
                                 Tamchekket
Rosso   Morguel   Nema
St Louis   Kaedi   Kiffa   THE ROAD
                 Leqceiba

                         River Senegal   Mali

Dakar   Senegal   River Niger

Preface

There was a young girl standing on a pier in the Senegal River, screaming. Her hands were clasped above her shaven head, there were two clean runnels in the dirt on her face where her tears ran down and her small bony body was rigid with all the fury a child can generate. I was in a dugout boat below the pier, waiting to be ferried across the river. My fellow passengers and I were transfixed by this girl. It was almost as if time and space had been momentarily petrified; there was no wide river as brown and heavy as oil sliding by to the nearby sea; there was no crowd of taxi drivers, village boys and black-marketeers pressing on the riverbank; and there was no customs post draped with bored customs men. There was only this girl and her terrible penetrating screams.

A woman, her mother, or elder sister perhaps, started to shake her violently, hitting her about the body as if she were dusting her down, but it only made the girl howl all the more. She was dragged to the side of the pier and the woman tried pushing her over, but the girl clung to the woman's dress with white-knuckled fists.

Someone in the boat stood up and shouted, 'Hey, leave her. Leave her alone.'

But the woman ignored him. She slapped the girl across the face, prised her fists from her dress and threw her into the river. The dark

11

waters closed over the girl's head, her screams cut short as if they had been guillotined. When she surfaced she stumbled to the bank, ripping her thin, doll-like dress from her body and sobbing air back into her lungs.

Slowly sound and vision returned; the jeering of the village boys on the bank; the hawking of the ferryman for more custom. There were seagulls overhead, circling in the air, browned with dust and dirt and stale heat, heavy and sullen like the river. The river was the frontier between Senegal and Mauritania. Frontiers in Africa always seem to be like this; tense, brooding places.

There must have been twenty of us in the dugout boat; fair-skinned Moors with bony faces and turbans wrapped round their heads, their eyes dark and distant; a few black mammas with baskets and babies; a small man with a nervous smile: he was from Guinea, he told me, and was now a tailor in Nouakchott, the capital of Mauritania; and a skinny American Peace Corps volunteer. He had been up-river for two years, teaching English in a village, and tomorrow he was flying back to New York. He looked worried and a little sad. Two years in a village upstream and then Manhattan was perhaps too much of a shock. In fact, we all looked a bit worried in the boat, except perhaps the Moors, but you could not tell what they were thinking. When the boat broke down halfway across the river nobody acknowledged it. Nobody acknowledged it when we started drifting rapidly downstream. And nobody acknowledged it when the ferryman eventually got the engine started again.

When we arrived on the far shore we had to wade a short way to the bank. We then made our way, a silent, lumbering group laden with luggage, to the Mauritanian immigration post where a man in a blue uniform could be seen, tilted back in a chair on the verandah, watching us approach.

I had never been to the Islamic Republic of Mauritania before and I was nervous and excited. I knew very little about the country, almost nothing. I knew that it was mostly desert, that it was Muslim and that the majority of the people who lived there were a people called the Moors and they had lots of camels. I had been to Africa many times before. I was always drawn back there, as if by some hidden force. I do not know how it is but people rarely visit Africa only once; one is drawn back in the same way as one is drawn back to one's family. At the moment I was interested in the big blank space on the far left-hand side of the map of Africa, called Mauritania. I wanted to open the window in that corner of the house and see what the view was like.

I had flown into Dakar, the capital of Senegal, a tall, metropolitan city of white apartment blocks and international hotels with a grid of steamy streets lying like gutters at their feet. It was very well equipped for an African city, but then it was not very African. It had been built by the French and its culture strove to be French. It was noisome and toilsome, the streets filled with filth and poverty and the large cool supermarkets filled with the rich and clean. The two worlds met at the supermarket door; a sudden blast of heat and outstretched hands to which one turned a blind eye.

I had a good hotel room, five storeys up and spacious, with a large double bed in the middle of it and red tiles on the floor, a set of French windows with shutters opening on to a balcony. The balcony looked out over the terracotta roof tiles of an old part of the city to the port and its busy, angular cranes; then the blue bay and then, on a clear day, the open sea. There was a ceiling fan and when this was turning the long cotton curtains across the balcony door stirred gently and the room would be cool without the necessity of air-conditioning.

The city from my balcony was nice in a continental way. In the early mornings the smell of freshly baked bread and market sounds would drift up to me from the streets. In the afternoons, when the heat was dense and sticky, the town lay slumbering, settled into siesta. And in the evenings the city put on a show that I would always watch. The low sun would cast a pink light on to the continental buildings and the air would hang still and thick. In the sky above the port and tall apartment blocks were a great many harriers, apparently about no other business than to enjoy the warm, uplifting currents of air. They would be circling and soaring, wing-tipping and falling, all the many hundreds of them scattered or entwined in spiralling play. I could sit, as I did, and watch the scene as an abstract whole, a liquid mould of smooth, gliding forms shifting this way, over to the right and out of view; or that, to the left of the tall port cranes. Or I could pick a single bird and follow with a close eye his steerage through the evening press of mates, his search for warmer air to rise and his tremendous speed picked up in a glorious downward dive to end with a little upward curve. But then, in the time of a brief lapse from my concentrated stare, it would be night or close enough to it for the distinction to be scant. The pink-faced buildings and the slatted terracotta roofs would now become grey and flat and the city would be formless but for the single meld of street and window lights that would begin to glimmer and glare. The sky, with a hint of mauve and wispy with smoke, would be empty, the harriers not suddenly leaving but mildly dissipating and so for a moment the city would breathe free. Or would it? A minute would pass, a black shape would flit past a window glow. Suddenly and silently a swarm of jerky, angular forms would take to the sky. Night was nigh, the domain of bats, bats two hands' span across, and through the night they would fly and squabble and cluster in trees, these creatures shy by day and sinister by night, or so they seemed to me on my balcony, in the company now of stars piercing the dark canopy, opening up the night.

From Rosso, the Mauritanian border town on the Senegal river, I took a minibus to Nouakchott, a journey of about two hundred kilometres. My map indicated that I would be passing through savannah; in fact the whole of the far south of Mauritania was shown as savannah, but it must have been an old map. There was no vegetation here, nothing in fact, just emptiness gently undulating to the horizon, a sandy plain strewn with knuckles of black rock.

We passed one or two villages, handfuls of small cement boxes with sand swept up against their sides like snowdrifts, and goats curled up against their walls. In one of these villages there was a police post and I knew the moment the policeman emerged that there was going to be a problem. He was small, swarthy, barefoot and bad-tempered and he decided to pick on me and the small tailor from the boat. I suppose we looked the most nervous. He went through my luggage, my pockets and my shoes, looking for illegally imported foreign currency. I had had to fill in a currency declaration form in Rosso and as it happened I had filled it in wrongly. I only got away with it because the policeman could not count very well. I had to count out my money for him, passing him each note. He fiddled with them sensually, putting them in neat piles. It took a long time to complete. Everybody stood watching. By the time we were free to leave the sun had set and the rest of the journey to Nouakchott was completed in darkness; three hours speeding through black space, staring at our reflections in the minibus windows.

PART ONE

NOUAKCHOTT

1

A good hotel

I did not like Nouakchott very much at first. It seemed a hard town to come to grips with, there was no shape or focus, no identity to be easily grasped and slotted into a notch. Sometimes it did not feel like a town at all, just a piece of desert that had been planted with houses, like an encampment. When I came to realise that in many ways it was a desert encampment I began to understand it and to like it a little better.

Before, there had been just a village here and a tented French military post. Quite why this spot had been chosen for the capital, where the Sahara desert meets the Atlantic ocean, was unclear to me. There was no natural port, no abundance of good water and no good road. Some say it was chosen for its favourable air, others that this was where in the past black Africa had met the Saharan Africa of the Moorish emirates. Others still maintained quite simply that Nouakchott was roughly half-way between the only two ports on this stretch of the coast – St Louis to the south in Senegal and Port Etienne, now known as Nouadhibou, in the north of Mauritania, two ports whose history dates back as far as the earliest visitations of the Portuguese and their trading with an unexplored Africa. However it was, the first houses built were a row of old-style apartment blocks with a small bungalow next to them. When

Mauritania gained independence from its French colonisers in 1960, the first president lived in the bungalow.

These buildings are now the centre of Nouakchott but in the autumn of their lives. Their paint is blotchy, their doors framed with years of dirt and grease and their green colonial shutters hang loosely on broken hinges. The president's bungalow is indistinguishable from its neighbours, all of them hung with washing and resounding to the wail of babies and the bleat of goats which wander in and out of their doors. Near these buildings are the children of independence, the many ministries housed in large bland blocks, the radio station, the police headquarters, the foreign embassies and the post office, all gathered close about the presidential palace. There is an even newer generation of buildings, a bank with marble steps and a huge Friday mosque to which more care and attention has been paid than the whole of the rest of the town. There is the odd coiffeur, a few upmarket Lebanese shops and restaurants and a large market complex for the people.

Amongst all this, many buildings were at varying stages of construction; many of them looked as if they had been that way for a long time: ministries still with the whitewashed windows of a building site, a hotel in full running order but with the top two floors still 'under construction'. The sand compounded the appearance of a building site. Sand is a problem in Nouakchott, sand and the elements. Most cities exclude nature – the elements are superfluous, slightly irritating things that make the pavements wet and necessitate the carrying of an umbrella. But the elements were as much a part of Nouakchott life as if it had been a small rural community. The large sand seas that lay around the town also entered it, larger dunes on the outskirts and smaller drifts towards the centre. The winds, coming fiercely across the desert as they did for much of the year, picked up a lot of sand and dust and brought them to the town. It was a part of life, on office floors, in each mouthful of rice, between the pages of books, under your fingernails and in your ears and eyes. Then, when it rained in Nouakchott, which was not very often, the town would flood as the drainage system failed, and the mayor and the Ministry of Works and Industry would argue over whose responsibility the drainage system was. And, of course, there was the heat. It dictated the times you worked, the times you slept and the times you did or did not go outside.

There were areas, or *quartiers* as they were called, that did manage to keep the elements at bay a little, as any self-respecting urban centre should. These were the *quartiers* of the rich and foreign. There was the *quartier de sécheresse*, so called because all who lived there had built their luxury villas from the proceeds of the Aid money that came into Mauritania when it was suffering from the devastating droughts of the 1970s and early '80s that afflicted the country and still do, though to a lesser extent now. There was the expatriate *quartier*, whose inhabitants lived very comfortably and mostly tax free, and there were other *quartiers* where the richer bureaucrats and businessmen lived in ill-fitting constructions of concrete and courtyard, all surrounded by a tall wall in front of which, more often than not, was a Mercedes or a Peugeot and a flea-bitten mutt, not looking nearly as fierce as the *très méchant chien* sign made out.

There were no street maps of Nouakchott and to me it was a random place. I heard references to *quartiers* and places I never discovered. Only once, long after I had left Mauritania, when I flew over the town, did it suddenly take shape. Then I saw how small it really was and I saw the vastness of the desert in which it was placed, a few kilometres from the long line of the Atlantic coast. It looked almost like a scattering of gravel on a beach. There were three roads, one to Rosso and the south, one to Nema and the east, and one to Atar and the north. As these roads left town they drew a good deal of it after them, gradually releasing poorer, shanty *quartiers* until there was just a string of shacks and houses, then a tent or two, then just empty rippling desert. It looked as though the town was being pulled like elastic in three different directions.

At first I wandered the streets, a lonely stranger in a town that did not seem to have strangers, a town in which it seemed everybody 'belonged', from the beggars on the corners to the expatriates beetling about in their tall overland vehicles. In the afternoons it was a place

21

of wind and stinging sand. There were the besieged outlines of buildings across a road, the occasional car about as if it were a lone explorer. It was a place of men wrapped up like secrets in turbans and cloaks and long baggy robes, a place into which I made brief, determined excursions only to return to my hotel room a short time later having found little to detain me. Later on I became trapped, as wanderers will in cities, by the ease of familiarity and the routine of survival. The world shrank around me, shrank to Mauritania, to Nouakchott, and to just my hotel and a few of the surrounding streets. Beyond was nothing, or nothing that could be contemplated. No, Mauritania was my hotel at first and my hotel was a good enough place.

The first night in Nouakchott I arrived tired and in darkness. I felt almost as if I was on a different planet, so strange and alien did the silent town of sand and village darkness seem. I was directed to a hotel near Nouakchott's second Friday mosque. I stepped down from the street through a low door to an interior dark and cramped like the galley of a deserted ship. A shiny face appeared in a pigeonhole window.

'Yes, what do you want?'

'A room, please.'

'Okay. Up the stairs, third on the left, number thirteen.' A key was thrust through the pigeonhole and the face disappeared.

There were low passageways of brown cardboard walls with doors set in them. Through another pigeonhole I caught a glimpse of a television set and the forms of people watching it. Then up a narrow, carpeted staircase smelling of mould and dust, along another corridor smelling of fly-spray with more doors and the murmur of voices behind them. Then into number thirteen, a bed with dirty sheets, a shower stinking of drains, a school desk, a plastic floor and a porthole window out on to darkness.

My hotel was the only cheap one in town, the sort of hotel in which everybody has at one time or another stayed, one of those hotels in which the outcasts, the troubled, the fortune-seekers and the wanderers of the world end up and lodge for a while as if it were a second home.

Sekouba was the name of the man who ran it. He was from Mali, though for the sake of convenience he had taken Mauritanian nationality. He, too, had been a wanderer and fortune-seeker. He had come to Nouakchott twenty years before, looking for work. After a spell in prison and a stint working at the hospital, he had come to the hotel. He had now been there for fifteen years and in those fifteen years he had not left Nouakchott once, barely even the *quartier* in which the hotel was. He was now the manager and to all intents and purposes the boss. The real boss, or *patron*, as bosses and men of substance and respect are known in Mauritania, lived on the top floor. He was a Moor who would appear each morning, shake hands with anyone who was about and take Sekouba aside to have quiet conversations with him. The *patron* had a selection of large women who lived with him upstairs. They would appear now and again at the bottom of the separate staircase that led from the top floor to the street and waddle over to his car to be ferried to the shops.

'But I am the one with the money,' Sekouba would say to me. 'Even the *patron* has to borrow from me sometimes.'

Sekouba was small and stocky with a determined face and an air of boyishness about him, though he must have been forty. He was sure of himself, sure that he knew the solution to all problems. It was only a question of looking at them logically, he said. Not that Sekouba had problems. He *never* had problems, just things that needed to be looked at logically.

'No, no,' he might say. 'The reason why you should pay your rent in advance – although I let you pay in arrears because paying in arrears shows trust and trust is very important, you know – is because if you imagine, for example, that my wife at home has cooked me a fish for my lunch and has paid for it with the money her brother got in compensation for the shoes he bought last week which fell to pieces a day later, and then when I add up the day's takings at the hotel and tell the *patron* that it is minus about the equivalent my wife's brother got in compensation for the shoes plus the cost of the fish my wife cooked for my lunch, if you think about it you will see that the principle involved in paying your rent in advance is equivalent approximately to the principle of paying for a fish for my lunch out of compensation for something that was not as good as it should have been. It's really quite simple if you look at it logically, you see.'

Sekouba was one of those people who either liked you or did not. Fortunately I fell on his liking side. Those who did not did not stay long. He ran the hotel with great authority and firmness and this he had to do, not just because the hotel was often like a railway station with people coming and going but because of his size and his youthful air and the fact that he was a black African – sometimes people did not realise he was the boss and treated him as an inferior.

The people thronging the halls and doorways were not all the flotsam and jetsam of travel. The reason why the hotel sometimes seemed like a railway station and also another reason why Sekouba had to be firm in his running of it was that it provided another service besides rooms to rent, and that was women. This service was provided very discreetly, so discreetly in fact that when I first arrived I was unaware of it and thought it pure coincidence that women kept popping into my room in the middle of the night only to back out again with 'Sorry, wrong number.'

The women came from the bars of Dakar. There were three of them and they were tough and beautiful, one a deep, oiled black, one nut-brown and one the almost transparent off-white of a seashell. Sometimes they were demure and chaste Muslim ladies with long, elegant dresses of expensive muslin and shawls covering their heads. At other times they were tight-skirted modern girls, full of brashness and coarse jokes, gold and jewellery flashing at their fingers and ears, but always they had the hard edge their business required that told you they gave nothing away, not a cigarette, not a smile.

Their customers were policemen and rich, cultivated Moors. The policemen were good friends of Sekouba's, as they would have to be, but the Moors were not. He put up with them and could be friendly to them when he wished, but never would he let them treat him as an inferior because he was a black African. He always made sure they knew that even though he was in their country, when they were in the hotel they were on his territory. They would put on an

24

air of camaraderie and compliance, hanging around the reception waiting patiently for Sekouba to allow them to go into the common room to talk to the women. Then they would disappear upstairs. When they appeared again they left the hotel as though hell was on their heels. Once when I came down in the morning I found a young Moor having breakfast with one of the women. She was no longer the fancy beauty of the night, just a large and merry girl. The Moor looked dishevelled and morose. For no reason at all he insisted upon paying for my breakfast, then he left without saying another word.

Not all the people who came to the hotel would get in, though. Occasionally the *patron* would come down to tell Sekouba that it was getting a bad reputation. Then Sekouba would turn away anyone but the most respectable-looking men and he turned them away with a firmness that ensured they never came back. Sometimes they would curse him and insult the hotel but Sekouba was unmoved.

'Oh, I can tell a real *patron*,' he would say dismissively, having turned away two young Moors, 'and I am not fooled by two little things like that.'

Sekouba lived in a house near the hotel. He took me there sometimes in the long hot afternoons and we would play dominoes and doze. He was married to a pretty Senegalese girl with whom he argued incessantly whenever she could be bothered to argue back. He rented the house from another Moor who kept a couple of rooms on the roof where he stocked expensive merchandise like televisions and videos, and sometimes he brought his mistresses there. Sekouba complained a lot about this, as he paid rent for the whole house. He hinted that the Moor worked for a government import company, and that was why he had so many expensive goods. Sekouba really had a thing against the Moors.

Sekouba had the biggest, flashiest ghetto blaster I have ever seen. It had eight speakers, equalisers and an array of buttons that could perform nearly any imaginable operation; the pushing of one triggered disco lights that flashed all over the machine as though take-off were imminent. He had bought it for a lot of money but unfortunately, during the transaction, someone had managed to drop the machine.

25

Now it required a good deal of hitting before it worked. I would sometimes find Sekouba in his room bent over the machine, hitting it again and again with a clenched fist, his face twisted up with concentration as if he were desperately trying to knock some sense into it. He was very proud of his machine, though, and had a framed photo of himself and his wife standing either side of it. They were dressed in their best, their hands were laid on top of it as though on the head of the child they had not yet produced.

Sekouba was a kind man and prided himself on being very fair to people. Many Malians came to Nouakchott in the search for work and finding none, they would seek out a fellow Malian who would be obliged to help them in their moneyless predicament. Sekouba, being a Malian of some substance, generally had one or two such people living on his hospitality at his house and at the hotel, too, there were various people who lodged or just hung about depending on his hospitality.

The small common room next to the reception was the hub of hotel life; there was nothing to do in Nouakchott in the evenings. The television was more or less permanently on but no one took much notice of it, lounging in the red, faded armchairs. The programmes were generally very serious though they sometimes raised a laugh, such as international boxing, especially when someone got knocked out, or one about a farmer in Senegal whose fields were infested with locusts, and there he was with a slingshot, trying to kill them one by one. There was a French detective series featuring an old man very hard of hearing who never failed to make Sekouba laugh. Each time the old man said, 'What? What's that you say?' he would writhe with giggles as if he was in pain. But mostly there were stern-faced Moors discussing important subjects who would gradually fade into a snowstorm unless someone got up to push the channel button again, something rarely done for a Moor.

People at the hotel came from all over the world. There were Filipinos and Japanese and French, and at one time a contingent of noisy, burly French soldiers who told us they were on their way to the wars in Chad. There was a tall Ethiopian who carried an air of

26

dignity and mystery about with him like a monk and was never heard to utter a word. There was a young Libyan who sat each evening in the common room, throwing disapproving looks at the women. A Lebanese couple stayed for a couple of weeks. They had fled the destruction of Beirut and had ended up in Nouakchott looking for work. The husband was old and grey, and his wife looked haggard beyond her years. They had a young son with them with beautiful long golden hair. He had screamed almost continuously from the moment he first set foot in the hotel. Sometimes his mother would scream back at him, then the father would shout at her and then the hotel would sound as if they had brought all the troubles of their country with them. There was an Algerian who always made a point of being very jolly. If he walked into the common room and the people there were quiet he would tell bad jokes at which everyone would feel obliged to laugh.

'Are you content? Good, good, it's very important to be content,' he would say to me each time he saw me.

A young Frenchman arrived with a beautiful Algerian wife, who looked just about as tough as they come. They were working for a Swedish company who owed them a lot of money but would not pay up unless they continued to work for them. They had been sent out to Mauritania to sell encyclopedias and had just come from passing the summer months in Atar, sweltering in temperatures of well over a hundred. They were now just waiting for their contract to terminate so that they could resume their real and much more lucrative business of selling art to the Arabs in London.

One night there was a terrible commotion upstairs accompanied by shouting and screaming. Everyone rushed up to see what was happening and found the Frenchman standing terrified on his bed with his wife chasing a mouse round the room, knocking furniture and encyclopedias in all directions in her efforts to squash the offending creature.

'Urgh, urgh, get him out of here, get him out!' he cried. 'I can't stand mice. Kill him!'

Everybody joined in the hunt until the mouse eventually took refuge in the wife's handbag, then escaped in the nick of time to run off down the corridor and disappear under the door of another room.

When the hotel was busy the common room would fill with people every evening, ringing with laughter and terrible jokes as the women held court and the Moors and the guests tried flirting with them. Conversations ranged from the long and ridiculous to short, defamatory remarks about the French and what they had not done for the countries, such as Mauritania, that they had colonised. On nights like that I preferred to go and sit in the street outside the door of the hotel. Other guests would come out now and again and I would chat to them for a while, or to the old man who guarded the *patron*'s car during the night. Sekouba would step out and say things like, 'Life can be tackled two ways. Either you go and look for it or you sit down and wait for it to come to you. What do you think?' and then disappear before I could give an answer. Lemine, the tea boy, would pop out with his tray of tea glasses from the small back room where he passed most of his life tuning a radio and pretending to run a restaurant. He was a very poor Moor from the southern province of the Guidimaka, and was Sekouba's 'boy', as servants were called. He was a gentle, simple man who had a wife and too many children

to feed and accepted his lowly status with ease. Only the small boy who was 'boy' for the *patron*'s family upstairs teased Lemine by calling him a slave. Then Lemine would get very angry and try to kick him; when his shoe flew off across the road Sekouba and I would try not to laugh. The boy would bolt up the staircase to the *patron*'s floor, where nobody from the hotel was allowed to venture.

One evening, when I was sitting outside trying to follow a long story Sekouba was telling me in his fast, garbled French about a well in Mali, a Frenchman and witchcraft, a small, handsome man in a smart suit, patent-leather shoes and carrying a briefcase appeared on the doorstep. He was a Tunisian, he announced, and he wished to stay in the hotel. The only problem was that he had no money. He and Sekouba went aside for a while to discuss the matter and after a short time Sekouba agreed to lodge him for nothing. On the ground floor, next to the toilet, there was a broom cupboard into which was squeezed a thin bed. The Tunisian was installed here but came out a short time later to complain about the many flies and ants, which were a part of life in the hotel. Finding that he was ignored, he returned to his broom cupboard and settled in with no more complaints.

At first no one else knew that the Tunisian had no money and because of his smart appearance assumed that he must be very rich – even Sekouba had thought at first that he must be a minister at least. He passed most of his time in the common room discussing highfalutin' subjects with the other guests with great authority, and flirting with the hotel women. At first they were very nice to him, they would get up to give him the best chairs and supply him with cigarettes. As it became apparent that he was broke, however, they ceased to be amused by his flattery, his jokes fell on stony ground and before long in their eyes he hardly existed. But other people made a point of providing him with cigarettes and coffee and Sekouba gave him small amounts of money to buy food. With this he bought bread which he would crush in a bowl, adding water before he ate it. This afforded great amusement to the other guests.

The Tunisian claimed he was a music professor and that he had

29

had to leave his country so suddenly there had been no time to bring anything with him. He said he could never return. Not surprisingly, the hotel ran with theories about his precipitate departure – he had been caught trying to seduce the president's daughter during a violin lesson; he had dipped his hand too deeply into the university coffers; and so on. He was certainly a resourceful man. Each morning he would go into the town to look for employment; I would see him sometimes in his smart suit, walking up and down the main street, deep in concentration. He went to the embassies to see if anybody wanted music lessons. He tried the university and the French Cultural Centre and then one day he turned up at the hotel with a famous Mauritanian singer. She was small and round and looked slightly disdainful; still, the Tunisian got her to burst into song in the common room, accompanied very competently by himself. He was beginning to get his finger into a few pies and the hotel women once again took to giving him the best seats. It looked as if at least one of Sekouba's dependants was going to pay off.

At other times the hotel would be quiet. The women would be off trying their luck in the bigger hotels, maybe, and there would be few guests. During one of these times a famous Malian musician came to stay. He was a great man who loved life and the world despite the way it had treated him. He had been on the road since the age of ten, when he had left his home in Timbuktou. He had played his guitar to a thousand audiences around the world but he was still not a rich man. He was tall, strong and handsome with a kind face, if a little sad. He was one of life's big jokers and he brought an air of magic and fun into any room he entered.

His music was a mixture of soulful American blues and the uplifting, swinging songs of Mali. He had not brought his guitar to Mauritania, he said, because 'the Mauritanian snow would ruin it', meaning the dust that permanently thickened the air. He found a child's guitar in the town, though, and often as we sat outside the door of the hotel in the evenings he would play the old guitar and sing his quiet, lovely songs. People walking down the street would look over on hearing this incongruous sound. When the *patron* and

30

his wives came down their stairs to go shopping they looked disapprovingly at him, but he did not mind. I doubt if he even noticed. He had had enough of noticing the prejudices of people round the world. He was happy with his music and happy to keep everyone chuckling with laughter as if it were a part of their breathing process.

2

Around town

The days passed very quickly in Nouakchott. Each one was much the same as the last and the evenings came close on the heels of the mornings. Early in the day I would go wandering in the town, trying to find things out about Mauritania and so perhaps get an idea of where I would go. There was not much use asking people at the hotel: their lives revolved around it and they knew even less about the country outside its doors than I did. I did not have much more success in the town. I would be given the name of somebody who, I was told, 'knew all about Mauritania'. Finding that 'somebody' could take an entire day as no one was sure where anything was in Nouakchott. All the institutions were known by their initials and everyone was very bad at giving directions.

'Oh, yes,' a couple of men sitting on a log outside the Post Office would say. 'The INRS is now incorporated into the RRST near to SLIM, opposite the MSS. Or is it now a part of BRGM?'

They would point in opposite directions; then, seeing where the other was pointing, each would point to the other's chosen direction. Realising that they were still at odds, they would sink back down to their log and talk about it for so long that I would give up and move on. When eventually, hot and frustrated, I did pin the somebody down, he would suggest that I would be better off going to SLIM behind the NMF, and so on it would go.

On one occasion I tried the American Embassy as a source of information, hoping it would have a library of English books. I found its huge complex behind the *quartier de sécheresse*, quite overshadowing the presidential palace. The embassy was one of the best-defended buildings I have ever seen in Africa. In fact it was so well defended that I never actually saw the main building, concealed as it was behind a tall white wall that positively bred electronic gadgetry and sophisticated types of flesh-ripping, impenetrable barbed wire growing along it like ivy. There were searchlights, warning signs and guard dogs, and the neat turf beneath the wall looked particularly menacing. The gate was a complex barbican of rooms and anterooms of thick plate glass, hissing and humming with pressurised air and surveillance gear. I did not even get as far as the squad of American marines who were the ambassador's personal guard: the Mauritanian 'front man' told me there was no information to be had from the American Embassy.

I often ended up in the Centre Culturel Français in the embassy *quartier* next to the International School. This area was only a matter of five or ten minutes' walk from my hotel and the marketplace, but it felt much further than that. It was the sort of area one could find in most cities of the world. Groups of European children met in bike gangs in the evenings, pretty French schoolgirls walked home swinging their satchels, and an almost continuous procession of the best in overland vehicles belted up and down the roads. The people who lived here were the Aid workers, the road builders, the telecommunication technicians, those who handed out the economic aid, the food and cash upon which the country was dependent, the muscle that supported the sick old man of Mauritania, that kept the nation on its feet. But I was not so interested in the nation of Mauritania as the country of Mauritania, the land of Moors and African tribes, of camels and camps and culture. My search for it would lead me away from the embassy area to the marketplace and my hotel.

In the late afternoons the centre of Nouakchott would come more

34

to life as the many ministries and bureaucratic organisations disgorged their squads of workers. The central market complex would regularly overspill its three-storey concrete building and merge with the hundreds of boys and buskers and small-time businessmen who lined the streets selling their wares. There were areas of cheap modern clothes from Thailand marked 'Made in France'. There were areas of traditional clothes-sellers; stalls and stalls of blue and white *bobos*, as the French called the long flowing *dra'a* the Moors wore, draped over a shirt and short baggy trousers. There were turbans of indigo and white and tie-dyed shawls and muslin dresses for the women. There were leather sandals from Italy and long leather belts, the ends of which, traditionally, hung down below the knees. There were tall, proud Senegalese men selling sunglasses and scent. There were boys with glass-topped cases of wristwatches, and pen- and paper-sellers. There were areas of the teeth-cleaning-stick sellers, and women who sold tobacco that lay drying on sacks to be crushed and sold in little halfpenny twists or larger bags of a month or two's supply. Under a large tree a knot of golden thread stitchers wove their intricate patterns on the hems of high-quality *bobos*. They wore glasses and worked inches from their noses. Then there were the scribes and the learned men with long grey beards, selling holy books and scripts of the Koran. There were mat-sellers and cushion-stuffers and a line of tall steel cupboards filled with cartons of American cigarettes. There was a corner of shoe-shiners and one or two cobblers who sat in the sun from dawn to dusk with needles and glue, and mounds of soles and sandal straps.

The market complex was also home to a sewing machine industry, rattling like a factory, its corridors deep in cuttings and frayed cotton ends. There seemed to be hundreds of shops for suitcases and materials and shawls, socks and more expensive shoes. The stalls of the artisans were down in the centre of the complex. They sold decorated Mauritanian smoking pipes and leather tobacco pouches. There were silversmiths and goldsmiths with intricately worked bracelets and necklaces, and women who sold shots of snuff, pinches of jasmine, incense, gum arabic and the treasured beads and *perles*

35

that the women wore to display their worth. From the top floor of the market three loudspeakers blasted three different popular Mauritanian songs, merging into a continuous mesmeric wail that kept everyone going through the long hot afternoons.

Behind the market complex was a large open space, where the big, long-distance trucks converged, hammocks, water *guerbas* and firewood slung beneath their chassis. They were laden with sacks of millet and Aid food and were preparing themselves, like an expedition, for a run to the regions and a profit for the merchants who had good connections with government agencies. The twenty-ton trucks were strewn at every angle, some idle and empty, the crew and stray sheep asleep beneath them, some revving with a team of mechanics clambering round the engine like monkeys, and some rolling recklessly fast towards the roads, scattering livestock and the marketeers who used the space as a public toilet.

Also here in this open space was the second-hand car market: rows of Peugeots and Landrovers in varying states of decay. In between them squatted circles of tough, gnarled Moors in from the desert, involved in serious bargaining, their *bobos* hitched over their shoulders leaving their long, pale arms free to gesticulate shock at the named prices. Their eyes were alight and full of desire, as if they had been buying camels, the old means of desert transport, now often replaced by the so-beloved British Landrover. Here too were the old men domino players, the storytellers with their circles of audience, and the odd marketplace madman, naked and abused by merry children. There were goats and camels, horses and carts and squads of white-helmeted soldiers. Gradually the dust was stirred up so that by the time the sun at last sank into pale evening, everyone packed up in a thin mist of dust laced with the dying heat of the day and the layers of second-hand air, waiting for a night-time of rejuvenation.

Now the roads running by the market moved with a procession of municipal minibuses that rang with '*cinquième, sixième,*' as the bus boys called out the *quartiers*. The roadsides as far as the eye could see in the dusty air were lined with people flagging them down. Mounting sand drifts and bumping into each other like dodgems at a fun fair, the buses ran down the street, past the army barracks trumpeting the flag-lowering ceremony, past the streets of *bobo*-washers and pressers pounding the bright blue material on stones with wooden mallets, down past areas of smithies and leather curers, past the people's mosque and then out into the *cinquième*, the infinite town of shanties and tents and lean-tos in which most of Nouakchott lived.

There were many beggars in the centre of Nouakchott, living in shacks of cardboard and hessian in any slightly private corner. Often they were young men curled up in the dust with their hopelessness, the blank look of fate on their faces. Many of them were cripples. It seemed almost that the fewer limbs the cripples had, the more they accepted their disability. One young woman was little more than a head with the gentlest of smiles sitting on top of a mass of unidentifiable, shrivelled limbs. She was placed each day in the shade beneath the Air Afrique signpost in the main street and seemed to be a rallying point for many of the cripples. They would sit round her and sometimes this group of people would seem the most sympathetic in the whole street, busy with serious-faced bureaucrats no doubt stressed by the problems of conflicting tribal and national obligations.

There was a sort of beggar who lived in the street outside my hotel. He had a wife and a baby and had constructed a small hut from plastic bags and cardboard boxes at the side of the street. He was not strictly a beggar, since he did not go out begging – the people who lived in the houses nearby sent him a bowl of rice each evening. In the morning the family would sit in the sand outside the hut. The man had his Koran which he read and the woman had her baby to feed. As the day advanced and the sun rose, the family would move over to the shade on the other side of the street and sit there until late afternoon when the sun would once again drive them across the street, back to their hut. This was life for the man and his family, a daily migration across the street and back, waiting for the evening when they could have their rice and go to bed. The man would smile at me each time I walked past. He had been a desert nomad but the drought had killed all his animals. Now he lived in Nouakchott and all he had was his wife and baby and his faith.

Each morning in my hotel room I would be woken around four or five o'clock by the call to prayers, amplified through loudspeakers at the top of the many minarets. The whole town would echo with

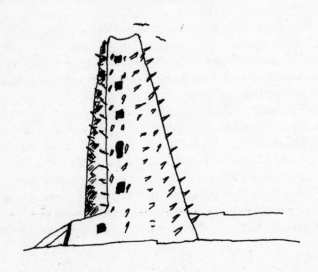

'Allah Akbar' and everybody would benefit from the prayers, whether he was an English infidel sound asleep, or not. The singing of Koranic verses would go on for an hour or two, a wavering sound joined now and again by a stronger chorus. In the grey pre-dawn light, halfway between sleep and wakefulness, it would merge with my dreams and float me towards a more decent hour when I would open my eyes and wake into a world that was all the more pleasant and tender for the hours it had already been a part of me. In the evening, the singing in the mosque would put the sun to bed with a choir of children's voices and the thin old voice of the muezzin.

3

Amadou, a friend

One day a young man called Amadou turned up at the hotel. He was a Malian and did not have very much money, so it was not long before he became another of Sekouba's dependants, moving out of the hotel to live in Sekouba's house.

Amadou came from Bamako, the capital of Mali, and had lived in the centre of Bamako all his life. There he had seen the affluence of the Western tourists and the Mercedes of the politicians. He had high ambitions for himself and decided to give up his education and look for work. West Africa was filled with youths of this sort, a whole generation wandering like a tribe of nomads from country to country, wheeling and dealing, looking for their 'main chance'. Most of them were looking for ways to get out of Africa, to reach Europe where the money and opportunities were. Most of them failed and either went home, resigning themselves to the lives of their fathers, or ended up in the big cities, sometimes turning to crime to support themselves.

But Amadou had only just started his search. He had done petty street business in Bamako long enough to save £400 with which he went in search of Europe. He had followed the inevitable trail, first west to the coasts of Gambia and Senegal, then northwards towards Europe. But northwards took him into Mauritania from which there was no northern exit since the border was closed due to the conflict between Morocco and the Polisario over sovereignty of the Spanish Sahara. At one time Mauritania, as well as Morocco, had laid claim to this piece of the western Sahara, said to be rich in minerals. The indigenous tribe, the Saouarhis, wanted independence, though, and a guerrilla war was fought by the Saouarhi Polisario Front. Mauritania was no match for these tough desert warriors and soon had to withdraw its claims, its economy virtually wrecked by the war. Morocco had now come to a stalemate with the Polisario over the issue, and the border remained closed. Now Mauritania was a trap and Nouakchott was a repository for all the youths who had made the same mistake as Amadou and now had no money with which to retrace their steps.

Amadou had the idea that he would go to Nouadhibou, Mauritania's main port and the last town before the northern border, there to try for a boat to take him to southern Spain. Sekouba had liked Amadou – indeed it was hard not to be attracted by his bright, open enthusiasm. He had told him he had got it all wrong and that if only he would do what he, Sekouba, suggested, it would be a much better thing for him. What Sekouba suggested was that Amadou should go into business with him. Amadou should give him the remainder of his money so he could have some new furniture made for the restaurant which Lemine the tea boy ran so hopelessly, then Amadou could be the manager of the new restaurant and they could split the profits.

'In six or seven months,' Sekouba said, 'you will have earned enough money to be able to go to Europe in style as surely as the money you now have would not last you a minute in Europe.'

Amadou had not hesitated in taking up this opportunity. He settled into Sekouba's house, waiting for the furniture to be finished and to start work in the restaurant. But the furniture was taking a very long time and Sekouba avoided the subject every time Amadou brought it up. After a while Amadou stopped mentioning it at all and soon he did not have a penny to his name and was dependent on Sekouba for everything, from his food and cigarettes to the washing of his clothes. As a result he spent most of his time lounging around the hotel, preferring that to sitting in Sekouba's house all on his own.

Amadou and I became good friends, because, as he put it, 'We are both adventurers.'

Every evening we would sit outside the hotel discussing the complexities of life. And at the moment Amadou found these quite amazing.

'I've spent my entire life up to now living in Bamako, getting up in the mornings, working a bit, meeting my friends, going out with girlfriends, popping home to eat, and I have never had a single worry and have been very happy. But now, my God, damn it,' he said to me often, 'I've left home to look for adventure and opportunity. I have long sleepless nights fretting about life. I get up and pace my room. I smoke too many cigarettes. What am I doing here, I ask myself. Have I made the right decision? Is this what life is about?'

When Amadou had first arrived, still fresh from Bamako, he had been one of the most light-spirited and enthusiastic of people. He came from a town I always think is like one big family – friendly, small Bamako, with its thieves who do not know the real meaning of crime, and its con-men who are so cheery you do not mind being conned by them. An African's city and my favourite city in Africa. When he had first arrived in Nouakchott everybody had been a delight to him, all his ideas and plans filling him with excitement. But in the space of a few weeks I saw him change, harden up with the rebuffs he met. I saw him become nervous and irritable and dejected sometimes. He was amazed by Nouakchott, amazed that nothing happened there, that there was no street life. He was amazed by the Moors.

'They are so serious,' he would say, 'too serious.' He thought them almost barbaric because he liked to be very Western.

'Their women smell very badly,' he said. 'I cannot stay here too long. Really, I would go mad.'

Amadou's eventual plan and hope was to go to New York – Europe was just a stepping stone to get there. He had a Malian friend who had gone to New York many years before and who had written to him telling him to come out. His friend had become a taxi driver

43

and had sent a photograph of himself leaning up against his yellow cab in central Manhattan, wearing cowboy boots and a baseball cap. Amadou worshipped the image. He loved New York and everything about it and he expected me to tell him how wonderful it was. But the New York he loved was not the one I knew, a hard jungle of fanatical workers and a price on everything from a smile to your mental health. I could not tell him how wonderful it was. It seemed to me that Amadou would be eaten up by New York, but I did not want to shatter his image. This was Amadou's chance to break away from the stagnation of post-colonial Africa and maybe make something of himself. He had as much right to his dream and his adventure as I did. We used to laugh at the fact that Westerners came to Africa to look for something deeper than capitalism, and Africans went to the West to look for money and capitalist opportunity.

Amadou had been brought up a good Muslim. He loved his parents and his home and he very much wanted to return there. He was only going away to make enough money to set up a business in Bamako and was tormented by the thought that he would fail, that he would have to return home still a poor man.

'Then what would I do? No woman would marry me. My friends would all have forgotten me. Oh God. Life is so difficult,' he exclaimed, laughing. Amadou laughed at everything when he had company. The one thing he could not handle was being alone.

'Then all my problems come down upon me and I get very depressed,' he would say.

But when he was on the street, surrounded by people, he felt more secure. Then, if someone was rude to him, he laughed. When people did bad things, he laughed at the ridiculousness of it all. He laughed when poor old Lemine tried kicking the boy from upstairs and his shoe flew off across the street, and he laughed at the Moors when they wandered up to the hotel to ask if they could buy a drink but in fact had come to see the women. He laughed at the terrible complexity of life as if it had been devised for just this reason and he held nothing against it.

We talked of anything and everything as we sat there outside the

44

hotel: Amadou loved to talk and I was his only friend in town. He told me that the last thing his mother had said to him when he left was, 'If you marry a Westerner, don't bother coming back,' and he told me of his adventures, like the time when he had gone to Algiers looking for a better education. The trip had been wasted – there were even more eager young men looking for education there than in Mali. When he had arrived over the border in the middle of the Sahara he had had to take a long detour in order to avoid paying police bribes, but then the local desert tribe, the Tuareg, had led him and his friends far out into the desert where they became so hungry and thirsty they had fought amongst themselves like animals and had had to buy water from the Tuareg at extortionate prices.

Amadou could always tell me something new on the intrigues of the hotel that unfolded daily.

'The Tunisian is putting his suit up for sale and Sekouba fancies the jacket.' Or ' "The Old One" is in hiding because two men are looking for him.'

The Old One, as he was known, was an old Malian *marabout* or holy man who was a permanent guest at the hotel. He was a charming old man who smiled continuously and cackled with great merriment at the misfortunes of life and the fixes people would get themselves into. He in turn was a source of irresistible amusement for Amadou, since nobody in the hotel got themselves into quite such fixes as the Old One himself. His function as *marabout*, at least in Nouakchott, was to make himself as much money as possible for the services he gave to people. Most of his services were small, cheap tasks like advising a man on whom he should marry by studying his divining stones, but one day the Old One decided to go for the big bucks. Finding two willing customers, he took a considerable amount of money from them, saying that he would double it over a three-day period. The following day Sekouba received three months' back rent from the Old One. Two days later two men were noticed standing at either end of the hotel street. They stood there all day, from dawn to dusk, smoking cigarettes. In the evening they came up to the hotel and asked if the Old One was there.

45

'No, he isn't,' said Sekouba. 'He has not been seen for two days.'

When the two men left and resumed their positions at either end of the street, Amadou was in fits of laughter.

'They've come to beat the Old One,' he said, 'because he has stolen their money.'

The next day the two men disappeared and a day later the Old One was back in residence. He went to his room and did not appear for another day.

'He's very scared,' said Amadou, with obvious glee. 'The police are looking for him.'

Of course it was not very hard for the police to find him, and for the next week or so the Old One was often seen going off with them in a car. But he always came back and he never ceased to smile pleasantly at everyone and everyone smiled back because he was so charming and because he was a *marabout* and *marabouts*, as everybody knew, were very holy men.

In such idle gossip our evenings passed. When I went to eat supper in one of the small restaurants near the hotel, Amadou would come with me. He had no money to buy supper and so would often go without. He would not let me pay for him.

Amadou's interest and enthusiasm began to centre more and more on Europe and America. He loved hearing me tell him of the bizarre things that went on there and he loved making incorrect comparisons between the two.

'In Europe, if a man sees a woman in the street whom he thinks is very beautiful, he cannot just go up to her and invite her to his house like we do in Bamako, can he? He must spend weeks getting to know her first and take her to dinner and bring her to meet his parents, isn't that right?' Amadou spent too much time reading the romantic Italian photo-story magazines that were all the rage in West Africa.

'But there is no real love in Africa,' he maintained. 'No African woman is "serious".'

I enjoyed being with Amadou because he was so simply honest with everybody and he made me laugh a lot, the way his honesty confused so many of the characters who turned up at the hotel. And I would quite unintentionally make him jump up and roar with laughter, too, and slap his thighs when I said things like, 'But I don't see the necessity of being a confirmed believer in God's existence if one has no proof of it.' We formed a small, warm friendship, only a little sadly, because we both knew that soon we would part and probably never see each other again. The people in the hotel, the women and the Moors who came to see them, gave us strange looks as they passed us squatting in the sand outside the hotel door. To them it was odd, even a little worrying, that two people of such different tribes should be such close companions.

4

Some Moors

Up until now my Nouakchott had been a town mostly inhabited by black Africans. There were a great many of them in Nouakchott, mostly from Mali and Senegal, but essentially Nouakchott was a Moorish town; it was just that so far the Moors had eluded me.

It did not help that I was so much amongst the black Africans – it was not easy to associate oneself with both. The two kept at a little distance from each other, their history of warfare and slavery interposing mistrust between them. The old nomadic tribes of the desert had traditionally preyed upon their black, agricultural neighbours like wolves upon flocks of sheep, and in turn the great kingdoms of West Africa had periodically overrun the fringes of the Sahara. And that history was not so long ago. In my hotel the Moors were talked of as though they were a single entity, as enemies tend to be. There were many mutterings about attempted coups and confrontations between black Africans and the police. The government was mentioned in gruff voices as an explanation for the bad state many black brothers found themselves in. There was never any open criticism in the hotel, though, and sedition never reared its head in any obvious form. The Moors and the black Africans had been neighbours for a long time. Trade and religion had passed between them for many centuries and on the edges, the two cultures

49

merged. They had to live with each other and were still trying to do so.

But people in Mauritania could still disappear behind bars for trying to rock the boat, so for me the Moors were still just 'the Moors', those who came to the hotel and those whom Sekouba disliked. They were the smart and handsome men who manned the offices in the town and trod its central streets. They were the roughened desert types with eagle noses and leathery skins who thronged the marketplace and the popular quarters. They were the men in robes and turbans who carried their shoulders as though bearing a banner that proclaimed their pride, the men who squatted in conspiratorial circles in the corners of their shops and seemed to look straight through me when I interrupted them. They were the boutique owners. Almost every door in Nouakchott opened on to a boutique, as any small shop or storage room or warehouse or any place of business was called. These were the same trading Moors I had seen in Gambia and Dakar, men born with business running in their veins, shrewd and determined merchants who played monopolies and certainties like cards stacked in their favour because they made sure they were the dealers of the hand.

Their boutiques varied from small-time retailers with anything for sale from only a barrel of oil and some gas lamps to the thousand-and-one small items available from the factories of China and Thailand, to the big-time wholesale men who hoarded sacks of rice and millet, two thousand plastic sandals or a thousand cartons of long-life milk that might only have to travel the distance of ten metres to the boutique on the other side of the street to make a worthwhile profit. They were the backbone of the real economy that kept the children fed and the cogs of profit turning.

It was not until towards the end of my stay in Nouakchott that I made some friends amongst the Moors. One of these was a man called Ismael. He came from a 'big tent' family, that is, a noble family. He was a Hassan, one of those descended from the fierce and unruly tribe of Yemeni Arabs who had swept across North Africa and then invaded the western Sahara in the thirteenth century and defeated the confederation of Berber tribes who had tried to resist them. It was the mixing of this Arab blood with the Berber tribes that produced the distinctive Moor, and it is their descendants who are known as the 'white Moors' as opposed to the 'black Moors' whose ancestry is long lost in a history of slavery and concubinage between the Berbers and the indigenous peoples of the western Sahara and West Africa. At first Ismael would have little of this.

'We are all Arabs,' he said to me, 'and our language, Hassaniyya, is pure Arabic.' He took it upon himself to educate me about Mauritania, to steer me away from the misconceptions he knew a Westerner would have about his country. The Moors were proud of their Arab blood.

Ismael had been brought up in the nomadic camps of the desert and although he had now lived in Nouakchott for a long time he was still essentially a desert man, slight, with skinny arms and long, elegant hands. One knew instinctively that he was as tough and durable as a leather cord. His own instincts were as sensitive as a fox's and he was wise and discerning in his dealings with other men, judging them more by their deeds than by their words. Ismael had an important and responsible job with the government, a job he felt more obliged to do than actually wanted to do. The government in Mauritania was, like the majority of regimes in Africa, military; some would say a military dictatorship, others would be more generous. Having this sort of job, his freedom was both restricted and confirmed, but he was a realist. He was well educated and had seen something of the world.

'There are those who think that by confronting our government you will only drive it further from democracy and that you must have patience and give it the space it needs to move slowly towards democracy,' he said. 'And then there are those who believe in confrontation. But that is still a dangerous pastime in Mauritania. We have come a long way, though. Now a man can expect at least to get some sort of trial. Before, there was not that guarantee.'

One evening Ismael took me to see some friends of his who lived on the outskirts of town. There were a couple of police roadblocks on the way but Ismael had only to show his face and we were allowed

through. Soon the town became little more than desert planted with solitary houses. We skirted sand dunes and potholes and then we came to a small cement box all on its own. An old man shook our hands and then went inside to sit in the one bare room with his wife. Neither of them moved or spoke for the rest of the evening; they just sat there, watching us through the door.

There were some thin mattresses laid outside on the sand. When we arrived there were two other men at the house, lounging on the mattresses in the fashion of Mauritania, shoeless and carefree. I perched ridiculously at first, then, when I was getting more the hang of things, draped myself across the mattresses and talked to a lopsided world. Two women served us with a relay of small glasses of tea and later a large dish of lamb and rice. We washed our hands and ate from the dish with our right hands only, in the correct Muslim way. There was a certain sense of formality about the proceedings although we ate, slurped our tea, flicked our cigarette ash and lounged about in utmost informality.

One of the men was a doctor-cum-businessman who lived most of the time in Saudi Arabia. He had no hint of desert about him, unlike Ismael, and had soft, puffy little hands. He talked of such things as nobility and the role of women.

'There are two mistakes you make in your country,' he said to me. 'You do not respect your nobility and you let yourself be ruled by women. Firstly your Queen, then your Margaret Thatcher. As a doctor I can tell you that women do not have the same physical and mental capabilities as a man.'

'Shut up,' Ismael said to him, laughing. 'You have been in Saudi Arabia for too long.'

But then Ismael in his turn became carried away over the subject of Israel and the Palestinians.

'My God, what would you do,' he said to me, accusingly, 'if your father and brother had been killed by Israeli planes while planting their crops in their fields, if their blood was running at your feet? You'd seek revenge. You'd want to kill the man who had done it, wouldn't you, huh, wouldn't you?'

The other man with us was a professor at the university. Whereas the doctor was easy-going, little concerned with anything like serious politics, and Ismael was only concerned in a hot, fiery way with injustice, this man was an academic politician and he wanted to tell me, a Westerner, a few things. He wanted to tell them to me pleasantly but he also wanted me to know that what he regarded as the imperialist West was almost entirely responsible for all the troubles in the Arab world. If I thought people like Gadaffi and the Ayatollah Khomeini were madmen, I should have a look at what the countries of the West were doing in some parts of the world. He was no fanatic but he burned with a grievance that the West should take a 'holier than thou' stance. He burned so much with this grievance that if he let himself he could hate the West with its smug technology, its air of superiority and righteousness.

'The West to us is culturally immature. It is only a child but a child that has a big and dangerous toy, its technology,' he said. But he did not hate the West. Indeed, he was a mild man and although his grievance burned, it burned deep below the surface and he only wanted me to see that there was another side, another view.

When he and the professor left, Ismael and I were on our own with the two women and the old couple in the house. The only light came from a gas lamp burning in the house behind us. It illuminated

one side of Ismael, who was wrapped in a blanket against the night-time chill, and shone in the faces of the two women who sat in front of us making tea. Beyond them the small sand dunes were just caught in its light, looming out of the darkness like ghosts. There was a profound silence and an even more profound darkness all about. The night sky was so clear it felt unnervingly close, as close as the desert hidden in the darkness beyond the lamplight, so close you had only to stretch out a hand and gather the stars as you might grains of sand.

'If you want to know what Mauritania is really about,' Ismael said, 'it is this.' With a sweep of his arm he indicated the dark emptiness. I knew just what he meant. I could feel the desert all around me. I could smell its musky space, and the quietness and peace of it seeped into my bones and unknotted all the complications and intrigues that are bred in cities.

'We are a desert people,' Ismael said to me from where he lay curled up like a babe in the womb. 'We are a free-spirited people. Freedom is the most important thing to us. Look at the clothes we wear,' he said, holding out his robe. 'They are loose and give the limbs plenty of freedom of movement and that is how we like to be. We may have to live in cities sometimes but we sleep outside the doors of our houses. We are not urban dwellers, as you can see by looking at Nouakchott,' he said, smiling cheerfully. 'It is hardly very urban.'

He talked about the desert a great deal that night and watched me as he spoke, with perhaps the slightest hint of reserve, even suspicion. He told me how his people gleaned a living from the harsh, infertile land that they loved because God had given it to them, and how it gave them life. He wanted the guest in his country to understand it, to understand perhaps that this was not just another poor African nation selling out to become Western and materialistic as fast as possible. Then he talked about the traditions of brotherhood and hospitality.

'Before,' he said, 'there were no strangers in the desert and today it is much the same. There are no hotels or restaurants – hospitality is the way of desert men and of Islam. Even if there were these places, nobody would go to them because if they did it would imply that they were bad men, men shunned by society, men who could find no hospitality.'

He gave me some advice.

'Do not be tempted to wear a *bobo* in the desert,' he said to me. 'Some American Aid-workers have done that and the people in the desert are suspicious of them. They do not trust people who try to hide their identity.'

We stayed sitting under the clear stars until quite late. The two women kept a relay of tea glasses coming. They were good-looking women with deep black eyes and soft complexions, demure and quiet for much of the time; but the way they fixed us with a frank and penetrating look belied that. They served Ismael and me as though we had been princes, then sat back and laughed in a way that made us a little embarrassed by our serious talk. They asked me to tell them about marriage in my country. When I told them that in England it is the family of the bride who must pay for the wedding, they shrieked with dismay and laughter.

'But that is too bad, too bad for the bride,' they said. 'Here the man must pay, and he must make it a big and expensive wedding or the girl will feel insulted and unsure of his intentions.'

Later Ismael drove me back to my hotel and in the hotel for the first time I felt a little stifled for air.

5

The fish market

I had been in the habit now and again of going to the fish market
on the beach outside Nouakchott. I would take one of the shared
taxis out there, small green Renaults seemingly held together more
by the determination of their drivers than by anything else. Generally
I would find myself wedged so firmly in the back seat between
two large mammas that I would not even be able to raise a hand
to wave a fly from my nose. We would shudder out past the hospital,
with its encampment of women and sick babies at its gates, past
the camps of 'urban nomads' constructed from the limbs of dead
taxis planted in the sand like modern sculptures and then we would
be out in the desert. Immediately a fierce wind would hit the side
of the taxi, veering it across the road to just miss a pick-up truck
returning from the fish market with twenty-five people standing
hugged together in the back, which fortunately had been on a
westward lurch itself at the same moment, and accordingly we did
not crash. To the west a dried flood plain of salt pans ran to a
line of sand dunes behind which was the sea. To the east was an
infinite wasteland of tin cans and piles of coarse gravel left by the
brick makers, who came out here to sieve fine sand for the bricks
that made up Nouakchott. Behind us the town quickly shrank to
a dirty brown line topped with an occasional minaret, and in front

the road ran true to where the desert met the sea.

At the fish market the few taxis somehow managed to get themselves into a mini traffic jam, the complexities of which were so great they required a great strategist to untangle it. A superfluity of great strategists making an attempt at it, though, it was a long time before one felt it safe enough to alight without the danger of being crushed between two theorists.

Along most of Mauritania's coast there was no break from the monotony of sand and sea, not a tree, hardly a point or spit of land, just a long slope surging with surf, the large Atlantic rollers breaking as suddenly as the chop of a meat cleaver when they hit the beach. Far out to sea many small wooden fishing boats, with the small brown bodies of their crews frantically pulling in or letting out nets, appeared at the tops of waves, then disappeared behind the ranks of green swell as if they were in a shooting gallery. Beyond the fishing boats the sky was stained yellow with Saharan dust. There was no horizon, just a glare and the mist of sea spray driven offshore by the strong wind.

The coast was a world of pale shades except where the road from town met the beach, where a sudden splurge of colour was dashed on to the sand like a throw of coloured beads. Here were all the mammas of town wrapped in their bright materials with twists of the stuff in their hair, all the fish merchants in long, stained robes and turbans, their gangs of fish-carrying labourers and skinny, naked boys untangling nets. And here were the hundreds of wooden fishing boats painted in red and white and blue, pulled up in lines above the beach, their prows jutting into the skies like the arms of worshippers.

There was a line of blood-spattered fish-mongers' tables, with choppers and blocks of wood. Three accurate strokes and off came fins, tails and heads. In front of them were lines of women selling small stacks of fish and townsfolk strolling up and down them, prodding and sniffing with an air of expertise. There were piles of sandy fish everywhere, skinny fish, long fish, spotty fish, fish as flat as plates, bloated fish with looks of surprise on their faces. There were hammerhead sharks and baby sharks. There were huge, coarse fish with rows of sharp teeth and mounds of hundreds of small, delicate pink fish. There was a continual procession of boys with crates on their heads, ferrying fish between the boats and the freezer plant behind the beach, blood and water streaming down their faces.

The fishing boats out at sea had to wait just short of the coast for a lull in the breaking waves before they could come in. Then, with a sudden surge from the outboard motors sunk in their floorboards, they powered forwards to hit the beach. Immediately men rushed to their aid. In a great, unified effort, they moved the boat up the beach, some sitting on one end and others pushing the unweighted end round, then sitting on that and pushing the front round, so that the boats moved up the beach leaving a mark like that of rattlesnakes

in the sand. Then the women and boys with crates converged on them and their catch was counted out by the market boss. He urged on the crews hauling in the boats, he cuffed small boys who got in the way and he pinched the best-looking fish from the women, who complained bitterly. The market overflowed into the sea and the sea washed up the beach and dragged away shoes and unguarded fish.

Most of the fishermen were Senegalese. Their boats were strong and heavy, the bottom half made from a single trunk of hollowed-out ebony and the top finished off with planks of local softwood. The smaller boats fished with lines and went out a day at a time; the bigger boats used nets and went far into the sea for a week or more. A young fisherman to whom I chatted one day told me that fishing with lines was hardly worth the money but that on the big boats you could make something worthwhile. Being at sea for a week, though, was hard. There was no shelter in the boats and no flat bottom on which to sleep well.

'But the air is good and pure out there,' he said, 'and you come back with many fish.'

One day I decided I would walk back from the market to Nouakchott along the beach. It was much further than I had thought. The cranes and buildings of Nouakchott's port, though they could be seen from the market, seemed reluctant to grow in size. The whole way along the beach thousands of large yellow crabs threw themselves into the surf at my approach. When eventually I arrived at the port it was evening and the sun had already dissolved into the veil of yellow dust hanging over the sea. The port was still five or six kilometres from town, so I hitched a ride in the back of a pick-up truck. It was the first time I had seen this side of town and it was the first time that I saw the extent of the huge *cinquième quartier*.

From a distance, across the flat plains of the desert, the quarter looked as if it was just a rougher part of the terrain. From closer to, it looked like a refugee camp but when I was inside it the first thing I noticed was how smart and neat everyone looked. *Bobos* were clean and well-starched, turbans were well placed on the head and men strolled around with their hands behind their backs seemingly oblivious to the vast world of poverty that lay around them. There were no houses in the quarter but hundreds, thousands of shacks and lean-tos, constructed from corrugated iron and scraps of wood and any piece of rubbish that could conceivably be utilised for roof or wall. The ground was littered with bones and dogs and excrement. People sat outside their shacks on mats, the open doors behind them revealing an empty, bare-earthed darkness. In the soft evening light the place did not seem too bad but I could imagine how it must be in the heat of day. The tin houses would be as hot as ovens, and the bare, scraped earth would reflect the heat and glare, creating an atmosphere of suffocating and oppressive proportions.

The *quartier* was built around a small mountain of Aid food sacks, in turn surrounded by barbed wire and guards. The people in the *cinquième* were desert people, victims of the devastating droughts of the 'seventies and early 'eighties that killed their animals, driving them to the towns and the Aid food. They knew how to keep themselves clean and organised in such conditions – in the desert they lived in tents with few possessions and water that had to be drawn from a well, often a long way away. They did not look unhappy to be away from the desert, did not look as if they were about to return. Here they had the advantages of more available water and consumer items and the huge pile of Aid food on their doorstep. They were nomads who had moved to 'greener pastures'.

The *cinquième* was joined to the more solid areas of Nouakchott by an umbilical cord of a meat market of flies. I was left there by my pick-up and as I walked back to my hotel I felt full of new vigour after my walk up the beach. Suddenly the world was a big place again and I knew I was ready to leave my cloistered life at the hotel, to step out into the desert.

PART TWO

FIRST STEPS INTO THE LAND OF THE MOORS

6

To Atar

I left my hotel at dawn. I was going to Atar, capital of the province of Adrar about four hundred and fifty kilometres northeast of Nouakchott. At dawn the sky was clear of dust and the air smelled fresh and invigorating. With my pack on my back I marched past the market towards the centre of town. It was still boarded up and lifeless except for a few figures fumbling over small charcoal fires beneath tarpaulins and moving stiffly amongst upturned tables and empty carts, wrapped in blankets against the cold. The time of year was December, the dry season, and although the days could be very hot the nights and early mornings were sometimes bitterly cold.

When I arrived at the taxi park for Atar it was deserted except for a group of men hunched around a small charcoal brazier. I joined them, our heads nearly touching, so close did we press to the heat of the coals. They had the look of early morning blankness upon their faces. An old man made some tea and handed the glasses round. They drank in three or four noisy sips, then lobbed the glasses back to the old man without a word and without raising their eyes from the coals.

Long-distance travel on the few roads of Mauritania was carried out in Peugeots with three rows of seats, a capacity for ten uncomfortable passengers. There would be two cars going to Atar that day, I was informed, but most of the passengers would not turn up until much later. The quiet early morning hours passed quickly and gradually the taxi park came to life. Towards ten o'clock the wind picked up as usual and before long the sky was grey again with dust and coveys of sand.

As I sat waiting I watched young Senegalese men drifting round the taxi park trying to sell cheap wares from Dakar. They knew all about the psychology of their business and were surprisingly successful, catching travellers in euphoric, spend-free moods. If someone once showed the slightest interest, the Senegalese would laugh and joke and the person would end up buying something in an offhand manner, as if just to humour these slightly tiresome people.

By mid-morning a full consignment of passengers for Atar had gathered and suddenly, on an unspoken word, they dived into the taxi, grabbing the best places. I was left to squeeze myself into a tiny gap on the back seat. I looked around at my fellow passengers. They were all Moors but there was nothing being given away here. Everyone was silent. They held their turbans and *bobos* up against their faces as though they wished to be anonymous and did not want to acknowledge the physical reality of being squeezed into a taxi in the taxi park.

After stopping to fill up with petrol we headed north and in no time at all we had left the last tents and shacks behind and were in the desert. The tarmac road was straight and well made. At first the desert was just a flat plain of pebbles, but soon small solitary dunes started to appear, perfect surreal sculptures creeping forever forwards before the wind. Sometimes one of these dunes would have crept across the road; now and again they would have joined forces to make small sand seas, completely blocking the road. Then we would have to make a detour and the driver would have to drive as fast as possible, swerving in and out of small bushes and rocks in order for our momentum to carry us across patches of soft sand. The first time we came to one of these sand seas, though, the driver drove straight into it, presumably with the idea that our speed would carry us across. He must have been a fool, as indeed the passengers muttered to each other when we came to the inevitable halt, sunk axle-deep in sand. We got out and dug and pushed but to no avail. Then we heard the growl of an approaching truck. We flagged it down and with its driver's help and a long piece of rope, we were easily pulled free, only to discover that now we had a puncture.

Contrary to what one would think, these various delays did not sour the humour of my fellow passengers, who already seemed quite sour, but rather livened them up. They rolled back their sleeves, kicked off their sandals and went to work with enthusiasm. The moment they stepped out of the car it was as if a robe of anonymity had been dropped. They laughed and joked and sympathised with the driver for the bad condition of the road. There was nothing but desert around us, the city was left behind, and I , too, felt a sudden thrill of freedom and camaraderie.

In the early afternoon we stopped at a small settlement of three windowless tin huts, the only sign of humanity we had so far seen. By now the wind had picked up considerably; the whole atmosphere seemed to be moving horizontally and the huts hissed like snakes with the sand being blown against them. When we got out of the taxi the wind caught at our clothes and unravelled badly adjusted turbans. We passed the greater part of the afternoon in one of the tin huts. The other taxi going to Atar that day turned up and its occupants joined us in our hut. Amongst these new arrivals was an odd and very intense man with small beady eyes. He came and sat virtually on top of me, pushing his face close to mine, almost overpowering me with the rich smell of his turban and his hot tobacco breath. He fired question after question at me and I found great difficulty in explaining to him what I was doing in Mauritania. He wanted concrete answers and the more confused I became the more fun he had playing to all the people in the room, an audience that he kept in the corner of his eye.

The tarmac road ended at this settlement. When the wind had died down we drove for the next four hours across an immense plain so flat and hard we could cruise at seventy or eighty kilometres an hour, the horizon an unchanging circle. Had it not been for the rumble of tyres and the whistling wind, one could easily have been misled into thinking we were stationary. We travelled in convoy with the other taxi. As the sun sank the tall plumes of dust rising behind each car turned purple. At that speed we would veer towards each other like boats racing across a still lake until sometimes we were so close we could almost reach from car to car, little rocks and clumps of dried grass zipping past between us. Then we would slowly draw apart until we were just tiny black dots to each other, two small points of racing humanity as insignificant on the vast plain as two ants crossing a tennis court.

When the sun disappeared the taxis stopped for prayers. Stepping out of the car, I found myself overcome with a sensation of the deepest release, as if the very texture of the world had sighed and closed its eyes to the commotion and clutter of life: all around me, other than the taxis and their occupants, was the purest of nothingness, a grand, humming silence, a natural void. The other men stood in a line and having touched their hands to the ground and performed the ablutions required before prayers, using the sand in place of water, they bowed down again and again, muttering their prayers, then sat for a while in meditation.

When we got back in our taxi we discovered there was someone missing. Ah, there he was, crouched behind the only obstacle in the entire landscape, a small bush quite a way off. When he had finished he wandered back to us very slowly, as if there were not nine people waiting for him.

The rest of the journey was a dark, exhausting blur fixed upon the bounding beams of our headlights. Vague hills appeared to the east, the plain broke from its rigidity to a land of sand drifts and small, scrubby hillocks, and then we hit a dirt road. The other taxi we left far behind shortly after it got dark. In our car we were silent except for one man who chanted the Koran continually, as if he were trying to preserve us from the fate our headlong plunge into swirling darkness seemed to predict. Later in the night I sensed we were rising. There was rock all about us, mountains rearing up to darken even further the dark sky. We descended into gullies and rose up again. We hit a wider and better road and sometime around midnight, we arrived in Atar.

The other passengers disembarked one by one at different places in the town and soon there was only myself and the driver left. He said nothing but a little later stopped in a large open space surrounded by the outlines of low buildings; in one of these was an open door illuminated by the yellow glow of an oil lamp. He unloaded my backpack from the back of the taxi and directed me towards the door.

'Maybe you can stay there,' he said, and was off, leaving me standing in the middle of the square with my bag at my feet like a new boy on his first day at school.

7

Atar, capital of Adrar

Entering the doorway, I found myself in a room with brown, crumbling walls, empty but for two mats on the ground and two men on the mats.

'Welcome, come in and sit down,' the face of a young black African said to me. 'How are you? Have you come from Nouakchott? Yes, sit down and be most welcome.'

I sat down and a couple of minutes with this friendly man left me feeling as comfortable and relaxed as if I had spent my entire life in Atar.

The other man was older, a Moor. He had a dirty white turban piled like old washing on top of his head and when he smiled revealed a scene of devastation where his teeth should have been. He had a friendly face that jumped about as though not quite sure just what expression might please most. He told me he was the *patron* of this establishment which, he explained, was a sort of restaurant.

'And I'm sure you would like something to eat after your long and tiring journey,' he said. 'And how is it?' he continued.

'How is what?' I asked.

'France.'

'Well, I'm not quite sure,' I replied. 'I'm English.'

'Ah, you're English, that's very good,' he smiled, rubbing his hands

71

together. 'Yes, I have many English friends. In fact I have many European friends.' He knew all about Europeans, he said, and liked them all. He took me through a door in the back of the room to get me some food and show me to a place where I could sleep. But first of all he showed me a collection of postcards that proved he did have many European friends. Sure enough, he was a popular man, with friends from as far away as London and Tokyo, even if those friends might have grown very old since they sent the cards.

I now found myself in a large room; rather it had ceased to be a room as its back wall was missing, and it opened on to a yard. It had a table with a dim light bulb hanging over it by a wire quite rigid with fly spots. The yard was formed by the backs of other buildings with niches in which sat large black pots and dumps of charcoal, and vats of water and washing. A half-broken wall extended a short way into the yard upon which were placed pieces of sheep or goat. The ground was sandy and muddy in the corner near the washing vats, and Mohammed showed me up a few steps in the back of one of the buildings to a small room – a deep pit with two poles across it, which was the toilet. I was shown another room which Mohammed explained was his but that for a reasonable sum I could rent it from him. There were two mattresses on the floor and many barrels of oil and sacks of rice. The far wall had partially fallen down where the floor had caved in slightly, and another room was revealed through the hole. I thanked him very much for giving up his room and we agreed on a price.

Mohammed set about scraping out the bottom of one of the big pots in the yard to get me some supper. As I was eating this a Frenchman walked in. He sat down next to me and Mohammed scraped out some more rice for his supper.

Jean was the Frenchman's name. He was a tall, powerful man with a full black beard and black eyes. He was a teacher in Nouadhibou, he told me, on his way back there after some leave spent in France. He had been in Mauritania for his military service, and like so many of the tough young Frenchmen who do their military service in Africa,

72

he could not see himself settling back into his own country, so when he had left the army he stayed in Africa to teach.

Although I was tired after my journey I did not go to bed for a long time. Mohammed produced some coffee and Jean produced a map of the region around Atar, a very detailed one, as large as the map I had of the whole country. Looking at it was like opening a book with a blank cover to discover inside a beautifully illustrated story. The desert suddenly came to life. What to me had been just great spaces, varying a little in shades of yellow and brown, became a land filled with canyons and plateaux and mountain ranges. There were long, wide valleys and gullies and great sand seas. There were paths and tracks criss-crossing as intricately as the marks beetles make on the slopes of sand dunes. There were oases and ancient sites, good wells and bad wells. Everything had a name, from the smallest hill to the plainest expanse of gravel. Desert was not just open reaches of desolation, after all. It was a land, someone's land, where there were places to go and things to see.

Jean and I got very excited, drinking our coffee and looking at the map. He had a week before he was due back at work in Nouadhibou so we made plans to go to all these places. We thought of camel rides to here, then by foot to there, then get a lift back here, and so on. Our imaginations were fired, our plans impracticable, but now we had the spirit of the thing and one way or another we were going to go to those places.

That night I slept badly in Mohammed's room. I had drunk too much coffee and it was too long since I had been without the comforts of the Western world, so I fretted about the cockroaches and the mice who frolicked round my mattress.

Next morning, while we were having breakfast, a woman came into the yard and started shouting at the young man who was Mohammed's helper.

'This man must come back with me to my house,' she yelled. 'He has come to me many times and slept with me and he thinks he can just walk out in the morning, but he can't do that, he must stay in my house and live with me.'

73

The young man looked embarrassed at first but as she went on he became angry.

'What a lie,' he said. 'What use would I have for an old wretch like you? Never would I sleep with one who is old enough to be my mother.'

Turning on Mohammed, the woman stormed, 'You, you keep him from me. I demand you release this man or give me some money in recompense.'

The mention of money had an abrupt effect on Mohammed. He turfed them both out and came back laughing.

'Oh, the things the young men get up to nowadays, rutting like rabbits with anything that comes along. Oh dear, what taste, what taste they have.'

After breakfast Jean went to look for a friend of his who was a teacher in Atar and I went out to look at the place. It was a close-knit town, huddled in on itself against the heat and glare of the desert with just a few long, wide thoroughfares, open expanses of hard, reddish earth blown over with sand running between the rows of low, rough-hewn reddish houses, their blue-painted doors shuttered as firmly as boxes. The smaller streets and alleyways that led off these thoroughfares were often deep in sand, with drifts blown up against doors that had not been opened for a long time. Sometimes there was so much sand in the alleyways I would find myself rising above the height of the houses. Then I would see across the jigsaw of homes and crumbling half-walls that surrounded each family yard. There would be chickens pecking amongst odd pots and pans and scraps and maybe an old woman asleep on a mat in the shade of a lean-to, her shawl pulled over her head. As I walked I would catch glimpses now and again of women appearing ahead of me, only to disappear a second later in the brown face of the town, some last trails of colourful material floating behind them. Sometimes, round a corner, I would come across a posse of children playing marbles. They would freeze and watch me as I passed. Then they would follow me for a while, whispering, 'Nasrani, Nasrani,' as if it were a secret word: 'Christian, Christian.' But other than those odd touches of humanity amongst the rubble and the sand drifts I was left alone with the sheep and goats lying in lines along the walls.

What of this capital of the Adrar, a region that was once the centre of the ancient fief of the Almoravids, those Sanhaja Berbers, those wild desert nomads who on a spur of religious zeal conquered and became lords not only of the whole of the western Sahara, but also of all of that which today is Morocco, of large parts of Northern Algeria and the Muslim lands in the south of Spain? What of them and what of this land, once the most powerful of the Moorish emirates, a land famed for its fierce warriors and great tribes who held out so long against the bloody 'pacification' of the French colonisers when their brothers further south had been defeated and were in alliance with the infidels? It was in this land that the final and cruel battle of the palm groves had been fought, it is from this land now that secret opposition to modern governments so often stems. But here about me this past magnificence and present turmoil were not apparent. They kept quiet behind humble doors, dispersed in the hearts of the people. Even the marketplace in the centre of town lacked conviction. But perhaps behind those impassive faces crowding the many boutiques, with their inevitable sacks of grain and blocks of salt and mass of Chinese hardware goods, one could glimpse a dormant warrior with a flair for fighting, a flair for freedom, for vendettas, for any reason good enough to mount a camel and brandish a gun once more.

The market itself was simple and poor: a few old tomatoes; some onions and carrots in small neat piles in front of patient mammas; boys standing in a line selling French baguettes on boxes, banging them together to dislodge the dust like someone warming their hands. In one long house built from stone like a shepherd's croft there were the artisans for whom Atar was renowned. But again they wore a humble face. There was no dash of brilliance here, no showmanship, just a gathering of gnarled and dirty men sitting on the earth surrounded by the scraps and pieces from which they made their trade. From these odd strips of camel hide and second-hand metal and piles of charcoal and hand-bellows and razor blades and natural paints, they produced their intricately patterned cushion covers, their fine and elegant smoking pipes, and penknives as sturdy and solid as lumps of lead. There was something in Atar, one felt; its history had a foundation but it was deceiving to the eye, run down, broken, closed and quiet.

I met Jean later on back at Mohammed's restaurant. In the afternoon we went to see a famous *marabout*. His house was in sharp contrast to the rest of the town, three tall, whitewashed villas rising up three floors, with balconies and verandahs and expanses of green roof tiles. All around the complex was a tall wall topped with broken bottles set in cement. At the foot of the grand front door a crowd of pilgrims sat, praying and meditating. Pilgrims came to see this *marabout* from far and wide and once, it was said, even a group of Japanese Muslims came to visit him.

Jean told me the *marabout* had four sons. The eldest, and so the one to inherit his father's position, had spent some years in America where he gained a reputation for wildness. He had by all accounts acquainted himself fully with the more decadent side of capitalist culture: fast cars, fast girls and the high life. But, having had his fill, he had come back to Mauritania and was now dutifully fulfilling his role as a religious adherent and was well on his way to gaining the same respect his father had. The second son was at this very moment following in his brother's footsteps and enjoying the fruits of America. The next son down Jean and I saw later in the day. His father had just bought him a new car, making him probably the only person in Atar to have a vehicle purely for leisure. We met him round a corner in one of the smaller streets. He executed a good hand-brake turn and then, gunning the engine, shot past us, leaving two deep tracers in the sand and scattering women and children to press themselves against the walls of houses. The women smiled after him in the way people do at a wayward but adorable child. As he passed I saw a pair of frantic eyes desperate to do something that might break him out of the fate of his family who were, to all intents and purposes, above the law. Maybe soon he, too, would be able to go to America to exorcise himself. The fourth son we saw as we stood outside the *marabout*'s house: a bright, cheeky child's face topped with locks of soft black hair. He was peering down from some crenellations on to the pilgrims at the front door. When he saw us looking at him he popped his head down out of view, as if he were playing hide-and-seek.

That evening Jean and I walked out of town to see the palm groves. There were supposedly forty thousand palm trees in Atar and its environs. It was from this wealth of dates, and the small plots of wheat and millet and vegetables that grew in their shade, that Atar had grown. The groves were thick, dark tangles of foliage surrounded by wire fencing to stop animals wandering amongst them. The land around them was as bare and barren as a moonscape, but the groves were lush, watered from the deep reserves of water that lay beneath Atar.

The man who had welcomed me to Mohammed's restaurant on the first night told us he would help us find a cheap Landrover to rent for our tour. Next morning we set off to the marketplace with him. He had only one leg and walked with the aid of a primitive crutch tucked under an arm powerful as a boxer's. We walked down the main street with our friend hobbling between us.

'Yes, it is a very good idea to make a tour of the oases around here,' he announced, as though he was a tour guide. 'And you will be very safe because white men are greatly respected here. Not like us black men. For us it is very dangerous.'

'Dangerous?' I enquired.

'Yes, very dangerous,' he said. 'The police, you know, do not like black men.'

'And what are you doing in Atar?'

'Oh, I came here looking for some business, but as you can see there is not much here, so I am waiting.'

'Waiting? Waiting for what?'

'Oh, I just wait, I just wait, you know.'

'Yes,' I said.

We were taken to a boutique near the market and introduced to its owner, a man called Moktar. He was small and bony with a thin, 'weasel' face. Outside his door was a Landrover, a very old Landrover. We shook hands with Moktar and everyone else in the boutique, as was the custom. Even people who were just passing in the street popped in to shake our hands and then stayed to see what we wanted of Moktar.

It was proposed that he should take us on a three- or four-day tour of the oases to the south of Atar. Jean inspected the Landrover, commenting on the state of its tyres and alluding to the possible state of its engine but Moktar professed complete faith in his vehicle. The bargaining over a price went on a long time. Many people came and joined in. At last, when it looked as if we would not come to an agreement, another Landrover pulled up and the driver told us he would take us for a lower price than Moktar was naming. This driver and his Landrover were as clean and well turned-out as Moktar and his Landrover were neglected and scruffy and their arrival immediately brought Moktar's price down to a very acceptable sum, so we shook hands with him and confirmed the mission.

Jean, who had not done his military service for nothing, took Moktar by the ear and said, 'We *won't* break down, will we? Because, you know, if we do, chop, chop, I shall cut off your ears.'

'No, no. We won't break down,' Moktar said, with a grin.

8

Oasis

A couple of miles outside Atar we broke down. Moktar smiled sheepishly and hopped out of the Landrover.

'Don't worry,' he said through the window. 'I'm a good mechanic.' He disappeared under the bonnet for a while with a rock from the roadside and hit things with it. Soon he was back in the driving seat.

'Watch,' he said, and sure enough, the engine fired first time and we were off.

'Here in the desert,' Moktar explained, 'it is not the surface of things that is important. It is what is beneath the surface that counts and my Landrover has a good engine.'

A couple of miles further on a particularly large bump in the road dislodged the steering console, which fell into Moktar's lap. This was easily enough fixed with a piece of string. Moktar continued to grin as he fixed it and Jean laughed. Moktar was all right. He did not look much, perhaps, but under the surface there was a resourceful desert man.

We were on our way to the Ksars of Adrar, the small oasis villages tucked away in the Adrar Massif, supplied by its subterranean stores of rainwater. These Ksars had for centuries been the retreat of nomads at the hottest times of year and during times of warfare. They were the hearts of their tribes, where their date palms were tended and

79

their children educated in the Koranic schools.

Just the word 'oasis' conjured up delectable visions, no doubt what Jean and I had in mind as we drove down the main piste south. Now and again big trucks would appear a long way off, small black points attached to tall plumes of dust that came nearer and nearer until, with a roar, they passed, leaving us hidden for a while in their wake. There were one or two fast Toyota landcruisers that spun past us, troops of roadworkers armed with picks and shovels clinging on in the back, looking sternly ahead as if going into battle.

We turned off this road after an hour and headed east towards some large black mountains. They were not as impressive as they should have been, for the wind once again was shrouding the world in a fine dust. Later we descended from the rocky uplands of Atar into the beginnings of a large valley where we encountered our first sand sea; a fifty-foot wall of sand being held at bay by three trees; behind this was a dunescape with small, gravelly valleys winding through it. We drove along these valleys and crested dunes with speed and spinning wheels. Oh yes, Moktar was enjoying himself, pitting his skill and his beloved Landrover against all this sand that tried so hard to claw us into its depths.

'You see,' he cried, above the roar of the engine. 'It's a good Landrover, no problems, no problems at all.'

At one time we came across some patches of millet and melons, a miraculous discovery, or so it seemed to me, for surely we had happened upon them by chance? There had been no indication of direction that I could see, no piste or car tyre tracks to follow. But Moktar hopped out and greeted the two men there as if he had been expecting to see them. They split melons for us to suck their green juicy insides and pulled up carrots for us to eat which were as fresh and crunchy as those grown in the cold, muddy fields back home. The place was called Touakiat. The millet, which I had been staring at in amazement, was a different colour on each stem. Each had been wrapped in a piece of material to prevent it being eaten by insects; each and every head of the crop so carefully wrapped up, like gifts.

We passed on up the valley, out of the dunes, and rolled like a boat across the slow, low waves of sand. Gradually the valley sides drew closer until they had almost pinched together and there we came across our first oasis, Toungad, its rocky houses almost indistinguishable from the walls except that each house was thatched with dry palm fronds. At the foot of the village was a long *palmerie*, quiet and still. We stopped only briefly to have some lunch. There were no people about but we were not alone. We already had a consignment of passengers in the back of the Landrover, men with sacks of grain and goats, who had been sitting in shaded spots in the desert waiting for people like us to happen along.

After we had shared a few tins of sardines and some bread and brewed some tea, Moktar went off in the Landrover to see some village people. Jean and I walked down into the *palmerie* to meet him on the far side and were at once engulfed in its welcoming freshness. Ragged palm fronds formed a canopy overhead shutting out the stark dryness of the desert. Beneath the trees was a mosaic of small plots of moist earth and the new green shoots of wheat. Putting my hand down I could feel a layer of coolness resting like a blanket on the newly tilled earth. Further down the path we came across a truck being loaded with palm fronds.

'Salam aleikum . . . le-bass . . . Yak le-bass,' we called to the men loading it up, and Jean went on with the formal greetings which were such an important and necessary part of any meeting between two people in Mauritania and which I had still to grasp.

'No evil . . . on you no evil . . . how are you . . . no evil, thank God . . . may you and yours remain safe . . . may nobody intend harm to you . . . may God give you strength and bless all your family', and so on – a long ritual, the main purpose of which was to give one time to size up one's opposite number, the same words being repeated again and again and even being reverted to later on if conversation flagged.

'You're welcome in our village,' the men said to us. 'Why don't you stay with us?'

'We can't. Our driver, Moktar, is waiting for us on the other side of the *palmerie*.'

'Ah, then you must go and may God go with you. We hope you have no problems with Moktar. His Landrover is old, you know. God protect you.'

When we found Moktar on the far side of the *palmerie* we saw that our passengers now numbered six with many sacks of grain and two goats.

'How's business?' Jean asked.

'No, no. These people just want a lift to Oujeft,' he answered shortly, unamused.

We stopped at two other villages that afternoon. One was Oujeft, a collection of stone houses on a barren hillside with the ancient Ksar lying in rubble at its feet. We stopped there only long enough to have some tea, crouched in a small two-sack boutique, swarms of flies crawling over us as we dripped with the oppressive heat. An old man sat opposite us, his proud, finely carved face and his old man's hair dyed blue from the indigo turban he wore.

'Take my turban,' he said to me. 'Here, take it. You cannot travel without a turban.'

But I turned him down. I did not feel 'desert' enough yet to don a turban.

The other village consisted of only two stone houses on another bare hillside. Here we were fed milk and tea while a line of children stood along a wall, staring at us with wide eyes. One half of our house was open to the desert and the other half was like a cave, with mats and wooden bowls and an open fire. The stone walls were blackened with soot and hung with tools and instruments as rudimentary as the neolithic hoes and bowls I had seen in the museum in Nouakchott. The two women of the house sat away from us in a corner, encouraging us to drink more and more milk, as if not to do so would be an insult. All the while they picked fleas from the heads of small children pinned in their ample laps.

We drove on that day through what were known as the Blacklands and the Whitelands. The Blacklands were the uplands of Adrar Massif, shattered mountains and plateaux and their deeply gouged drainage systems of rock-clogged gullies; the upland plains were deserts of evenly strewn black rubble across which we travelled at a tortuously slow pace. Then suddenly we saw the Whitelands, the antithesis in every sense to the Blacklands. These were the lands of the ergs and rags, the vast sand seas that raged about the massif and the pebbly plains of the desert. Below us they laid siege to the massif; waves and waves of dunes coming from beyond the horizon, washing up against the hard black rock, climbing up the mountainsides, caressing them in drifting, mounting ripples of windblown sand. It was like the coming together of coal and cream. They were so beautiful and perfect in design, the sand dunes, I wanted to reach out and touch them, run my hand down their smooth sides to ensure their reality. But coming to grips with the work of the master hand of the wind is something that cannot be done. You can dig your hands into them, roll and play in them, but never can you encompass the beauty of them as seen from afar.

We passed down into the Whitelands, Moktar somehow finding a route through, now and again getting out to have a look about him. The sun sank and the dunes became grainy and luminous in the dusk and as we drove it seemed that we were floating, semiconscious, on the waves of a dream.

When we arrived in the village of Joale it was almost dark. I could just distinguish the few stone houses scattered on a rubble-strewn hillside. There were groups of goats lying in between them and two camels peering over a stone wall. Moktar had some family in this village, so we were given a warm welcome: everybody, from the smallest boy to the oldest man, came out to shake our hands. We passed a quiet night with the chief of the village and his family. His house was simple, like the one we had stopped at earlier in the day, and smelled strongly of goats and rancid butter. The chief was a shy man whose face was partially eaten away by some disease, but he did not seem ugly.

Moktar was authoritative. He lay down on the mats and cushions and ordered the woman of the house about. A chicken was slaughtered and prepared for our supper. The chief fussed about, making sure we were comfortable, and when the food came he would not partake of it, wanting us to have our fill before he gave the remains to the children. His wife sat in a corner, petting a child at her breast and laughing gently at anything we said. As the candles burned low and went out one by one, the children fell asleep at their posts in front of us where they had been sitting all evening, watching us as intently as they would a television set. The mother threw a blanket over them where they lay. When at last we were plunged into complete darkness as the last candle burned out, we two were taken to another house to sleep and Moktar went off to sleep elsewhere.

The house we slept in, a *tegit*, was a perfect dome constructed from dried grass; we had to crawl in through a small round door at its base. We snuggled down in hairy blankets and drifted to sleep to the coughing of the goats and the murmur of the village about us. Next morning I woke in the grey light before dawn to find the village chief sitting at my feet brewing some tea. I blinked at him over my blanket and he smiled back at me but said nothing, just continuing his careful preparation of the tea.

Whilst Jean and I were drinking, Jean told me that Joale was a village of *marabouts*, descendants of the Berbers who, having been defeated by the Yemeni Arabs when they invaded the western Sahara in the thirteenth century, had given up the way of the sword for the way of the book.

'They were the spiritual aristocracy,' he went on to tell me, 'and traditionally they were the counsellors and judges and healers for the Hassan warriors who protected them in exchange for this and for the education of their children.

'There is a rigid caste system among the Moors, starting with the Hassan warriors and the *marabouts*. Then come the Zenaga, from less notable Berber families. They are tributaries to the Hassans and *marabouts* and are often animal herders. These first three castes are called the Beidanes, the white Moors. Then come the lower castes. The Harratin are the black Moors, descendants of the original inhabitants of the western Sahara, enslaved by the Berbers when they came from the north, but long ago freed. They are now tributaries to the Beidanes and cultivate the oases and the lands of the Sahel.

The Abid were slaves proper up until 1970, when slavery was abolished. They put up a great fuss about being freed because they did not want to be forcibly removed from the families they had been a part of for perhaps many centuries. It meant they would be ejected into an uncertain, jobless, post-colonial world.

'Then there are the Igaouene bards, who are slightly feared for their sharp wit and manipulative skills; the Maallemine, who, being artisans, are traditionally not held in high esteem; the Nemadi, who were nomadic hunter-gatherers up until recently when there was no game left to hunt; and the Imraguen, who are fishermen on the coast south of Nouadhibou. The many black African tribes who live in the far south of the country do not come into the Moorish caste system but are traditionally regarded as inferior to all Moors.

'The system is not as strong as it used to be,' Jean told me; 'for instance, the Harratin have even become quite powerful and some of them are generals and judges. It is still there, though, most definitely still there.'

When I stepped out of the *tegit* later on, I stepped into a rejuvenated world, everything as fresh and bright as a newly honed knife-edge

and the village already on the move. Boys were herding goats out, a man was leading two young camels, and women were sweeping out their homes, shaking mats and pounding millet. I went for a short walk with the village chief up the hill behind the village.

'We don't have many strangers coming here,' he told me. 'Once a month a Landrover with medicine comes, but other than that it is only people like Moktar who come.'

We stood at the top of the hill looking over the village to a sand sea that stretched away below it. What a joy it must be to wake up each morning to this golden view. The village chief was delighted to see my appreciation of it. He was delighted, it seemed, that Jean and I had come to his village and he had accepted us into it with the grace with which travellers are accepted into a monastery. We had been a part of his family for a night. He wanted nothing from us, not conversation or information, for he was happy with what he had.

'This is a good village,' he said. 'We have very little but we are very happy.'

I could see Moktar preparing the Landrover for our departure so we walked back down the hill towards him. We had with us now in the back of the Landrover quite a collection of new people: three men with four sheep; a woman of Herculean proportions, dressed in black with a tiny baby cradled in her powerful arms; and a very serious eight-year-old man who shook our hands with great dignity. He was being sent to live in Atar so that he could attend school.

The chief thanked us for coming to his village and his people waved us on our way. We drove all morning, back through the sand sea, a different, enlivened scene this morning, shaded from different angles, shaped in more rigid light. We passed a mountain almost entirely engulfed in sand on one side. We rose up to the plateaux again where two of the men got out and strolled off into the emptiness with sacks on their heads as if they were in a high street. We passed Oujeft once again and then, after midday, we came to another of those wide, sheer valleys with a wash of sand flowing on its bed. At its far end it opened out and the sand flooded to a distant, shimmering plain with the vague dark humps of sand sea on its horizon. Immediately below us, where the valley drew in tight, was a long drawn-out village with a large *palmerie* pressed against the sheer side. This was the Ksar of Mhaireth. Moktar had some friends here and we were installed in their *tegit*, a particularly large one, the dried grass woven tightly and neatly like wickerwork and one long pole holding it up in the middle. An old man sat in the light of the small door, mushing dates in his hand, little worms of fruit escaping between his fingers. Inside there were three or four young men and we passed the afternoon with them, lying idly and comfortably on woollen rugs and cushions.

Jean entertained the hut with his innumerable questions, the how fars, how muches, how highs, how lows, of camels and hills and Ksars: he had ideas of bringing tourists to the Adrar and charging them handsomely for it. The men loved his questions; they loved hard facts and plans, especially plans to do with making money. One of them set about the making of tea.

Tea, and the making of it, is an important part of Mauritanian life, a ritual almost, round which Moorish society gathers to pass the long, hot hours of inactivity each day. It is the fire hearth round which families spend the evenings, it is the peace pipe over which strangers meet and talk, it is the board where business and the state of the tribe are discussed, it is a central core to life and so being it is always performed with great reverence in the correct and traditional ways. There are always, in any house, no matter how poor, the correct implements for the business: a shiny steel tray, a small tin teapot, two or three tiny glasses, a tin of tea and a leather sack with a rock of sugar in it.

The young man who was to make our tea set about preparing all these implements. A hot coal was sent for to light the charcoal brazier. A dish for water slops was procured. Everything was washed of the dust that lay on it. When all was ready and laid out before him like an altar, he sat back for a while and composed himself. Then, rolling up his sleeves, he went to work like a surgeon. The process was long and complex. The tea was washed, water was heated in the teapot, chunks of sugar were deftly cracked from the rock with the bottom of a tea glass and the coals were fanned with a sandal from the doorway. The tea, when it had brewed for a good long while and large chunks of sugar had been added, was poured into the glasses from a great height, a thin steaming stream of gold cut short with a deft twitch of the fingers. The tea was mixed over and over again back into the pot. It was mixed again and again into the glasses until

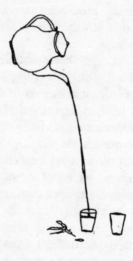

a respectable amount of froth had developed. There were times of little work and there were times when the young man's hands flew about the operations like a conductor. There were tastings, extra heatings and mixings. A sprig of mint was added, a little more sugar, and all the implements, including the outsides of the glasses containing the froth, were again washed before the tea could be served. Then all was ready. The tea had brewed down to a thick, sweet, dark essence and each person in the room would get an inch of this, starting with those of most importance like guests and the elderly, and ending with the young and the women. The tea would go down in a couple of noisy slurps and the glass, with its froth still intact, would be sent spinning back across the floor. This process was performed three times, using the same tea leaves. It could take anything from half an hour to three hours and it could be performed skilfully or not so skilfully. It drew one's attention, the therapeutic dance of the hands, the dash and verve of the operator, and one was kept on the right side of boredom throughout the long, hot afternoons.

Having passed the afternoon in such a fashion I stepped outside the *tegit*. I walked up to one end of the village and looked at its well-constructed houses; small mud-brick and cement boxes with no windows and firmly shut doors. There was nobody about, so I climbed up the steep side of the valley. The evening view from where I sat down was obscured in the dusty atmosphere, but I could see the sweep of sand on the valley floor, dotted here and there with *tegits* looking like pieces of flotsam. Soon I saw that the young man who had made the tea was climbing up to me. When he reached me he introduced himself as Ibrahima. He had a round, cheery face, quite shiny with good health. We lit cigarettes that burned like firecrackers in the strong wind, and I asked him why the Ksar was so deserted.

'Oh, there's nobody in the Ksars at this time of year,' he replied. 'You've come at the wrong time. All you'll find are old people and children and servants.'

'What are you doing here, then?' I asked.

'I'm a student in Nouakchott. I'm just here for a short holiday. The best time of year to be in the Ksars is the Gaytna, the date harvest. Then you wouldn't believe it. All the houses are full and the desert around is full of nomads' camps. There is great merriment and many marriages and arguments and divorces,' he laughed. 'Everyone comes together and exchanges their news of the year. It is a good time, the Gaytna, it's our time to forget our worries and enjoy ourselves.

'But of course the Ksars are not what they used to be,' he continued more seriously. 'The Adrar has changed. No rain, you know. Now there are few real nomads left and those there are do not stay here much, they are off down south or up north to places where there is some grazing. Before, you would have seen huge herds of camels and cattle in the Adrar but now, well, camels are becoming a rare sight. No, the people from these Ksars now mostly live in the big towns. There is only a small number of animal herders left. But they are beautiful places, the Ksars, so calm after the big towns. We treasure them greatly.' And he went on to ask what I was doing in Mauritania, and laughed because it seemed so strange to him that I should go wandering in someone else's country on my own.

'That is not something that I could do,' he said. 'It must be very dangerous.' And I, in my turn, laughed, because Mauritania was about the safest place I had ever been to.

'Do you think someone is going to steal from me tonight in this village?' I asked him.

'Oh, no,' he said, slightly offended. 'Never would anybody steal in this village, never.'

'Well, there you are,' I said. 'It's not dangerous.'

'Ah yes, but you know the people here are good people. Not everyone is the same. Down south they are different. You want to be careful there.'

We spent that night in the big *tegit*. Jean was teaching me how to play chess and so the evening passed in deep strategic thought, Ibrahima, Moktar and the other men crowding round us, watching every move with the deepest interest, though they did not know the game of chess. When, each time, Jean beat me, they would laugh at the brilliance of the game and Moktar would say, 'Ah, he's too good. He's a very clever man, very clever.'

We slept that night in a line, close together, with blankets pulled over our heads, like a row of corpses.

I was woken long before dawn next day by a continuous thump, thumping. It continued all the time Moktar made a quick tea after the others had woken, and when I went outside I found an old lady crushing date stones. She placed each one on a flat rock, then brought a big stone down on top of it, thump, thump. She was a very old lady with misty eyes and a face as smoothly wrinkled as the side of a sand dune; when she looked up at me watching her and smiled, the whole set of brown wrinkles stretched like toffee. The date nuts were being crushed to be fed to the goats, Ibrahima told me. I asked him if I could photograph her: she looked so handsome and tranquil. The old lady looked briefly up at my camera, then looked back down again at her work, as if I was not there. As it happens, I got the exposure wrong, so the best picture I have of her is in my mind; a grandmother of the Ksars, unconcerned with anything but what lay around her.

Before we left that morning, and while Moktar was fixing a puncture that had appeared overnight, Ibrahima took Jean and me to see what he described as a lake. In fact it was just a small pond tucked away in the *palmerie* against the valley side, left over from the last of the floods which had flowed through the valley in the rainy season. They had had good rains this year, the first for many years. There were two donkeys standing in its sky-blue water, puffy white clouds rippling at their legs.

Back in the Landrover, as I was sitting waiting for our departure, a young girl caught my eye in the crowd of people milling round us. She was the most beautiful thing I had seen for a long time. She wore a Red Riding Hood cape pulled over her head, and her face, syrupy brown and as fresh and charming as any spring bloom, held my gaze in a way more noticeable than was polite. Her eyes were large and in their dark, secretive depths I caught a gleam, as she stared defiantly back at me, that said, 'I know I am becoming a woman now and can tease such men as you because you stare at me so.' Then she stepped up to the Landrover window and peered in, all grinning teeth and inquisitiveness. I was very happy to find that she was coming with us.

When we set off from Mhaireth, the old lady was still cracking date stones. In the back we had a merry party; Ibrahima, the large strong lady clasping her tiny baby, the serious young boy and the beautiful girl. When we got stuck a few hours later, going up a sandy rise in a windblown wilderness, everyone piled out happily and pushed and dug with their hands. It took a long time and all of Moktar's skill to get us up the rise. Eventually, he just managed to get one wheel on to an outcrop of rock near the top, and with the traction of this and all of us pushing, he made it. We cried out our exhilaration, Ibrahima flipped himself over in a handstand, the strong lady clapped her hands, the young girl hopped into the back of the Landrover and stood there smiling down at us like a princess, and Moktar and the boy looked proud and embarrassed.

Soon after this we came to a canyon, a huge zigzagging crack in the earth's crust. For once there was no wind and so the world was displayed to us in all its clear, crystalline beauty: the sky was a dark blue with infinite depth and the side of the canyon fell away from us in sheer, craggy steps. Moktar drove carefully down the winding track but Jean and I went on foot. We felt like giants, filled with euphoria, as we bounded down the rocks. Down in the bottom of the canyon was a different world, a quiet, private place surrounded by the monumental tumblings of rock stacked and balanced in such precipitous fashion that one felt to remove the smallest stone would set in motion a landslide that would bring the whole canyon in upon us. The canyon soon stepped down to a deeper canyon which was met in turn by many brother canyons, then slowly its great width tapered to a thin gorge caught between the two walls like a vice. Here, at the foot of the gorge on a wash of fine white sand, was the oasis of Tergit; I could just see the tops of its tall palm trees winding into the depths of the mountains.

Carrying our boxes of food supplies as if on an expedition, we left the Landrover and made straight for the gorge, following a path to a tiny stream. The mountains closed in around us and we found ourselves in a dim jungle of tall palm trunks and thick, ferny undergrowth, a thin strip of sky overhead. We set our baggage down under an overhanging cliff matted with lichen and little stalactites that dripped with water. Under one of the more steady drips was placed a bucket and from this we each quenched our thirst with a draught of icy cool water that tasted delicious and earthy from the rock of the mountains from whose deepest confines it had percolated.

The floor of the gorge was covered in grasses and mosses and at the far and final end, hidden like a treasure in the thick foliage and bending bows of the palms, we found a spring and a pool of warm water. The young boy and I jumped in and scrubbed the dust and sweat of the journey from our bodies. Later, returning all red and tender to the others, I found them settling in comfortably under the cliff face, making tea and stretching out on mats. Jean and I played more chess and I took my first and last game off him, inspired perhaps by this enchanted Garden of Eden.

When dusk began to close in, Jean and I decided to go for a walk into the mountains. We climbed up and up, running and leaping from boulder to boulder, throwing ourselves carelessly at the mountainside. We crested false horizon after false horizon and we leapt, in our mad exhilaration, deep and dangerous crevasses, landing on the far side on all fours with a rush of adrenalin. Our spirits were high, we wanted to feast on this magnificent barren land. We stood on high crests and cried out, hearing our echoes come back from distant peaks and cliff faces, five, six, seven times. We indulged ourselves in the rock, felt its textures, marvelled at its shapes and ridiculous tumblings, we smelled its baked dryness. Then Jean caught sight of a young camel, and suddenly we were two small boys stalking an enemy, our friends and the gorge for the time being forgotten. The camel was wary, though, and we soon lost him. The sun sank behind a mountain and, spent, we began to descend. We went down fast, dangerously fast, but we did not care, we were invincible. Soon we saw the head of the gorge and slipping quickly into it, we found ourselves down in the darkness of night.

That day was 31 December. Jean and I had bought a sheep from Tergit to celebrate the New Year and Moktar and Ibrahima arranged for the cooking of it in the village. The first dish of meat – I say first, because there were many – was served to Jean, Moktar and myself alone, a large platter of all the choicest pieces. It was almost pitch dark by now, so we ate by torchlight, tearing into the greasy flesh with our teeth and hands as though we had not eaten for days, cracking the bones to suck out the marrow. We sliced open the large liver, revealing its pink succulence and let pieces of it slither down

93

our throats. We ripped the skin from the ribs and chewed the gristle and tendons until they were swallowable. Then we joined the others and got through two more dishes, one of boiled meat on top of a mound of couscous, one just a huge mound of boiled intestines which Moktar, Ibrahima and the boy savoured most of all. We ate and we overate, filling ourselves until we slumped back and laughed. Tea was continually on the make. The strong lady and the beautiful girl sat with us but a little apart, reaching for their share. The older woman laughed and joked with us but the beautiful girl was silent, smiling to herself as though she thought men the most ridiculous things. The more we ate the more noisy and riotous Moktar and Ibrahima became, like drunks, intoxicated with meat. Jean played the fool, jumping up, pounding the ground with a long piece of wood and clapping his hands as village women do when they are pounding grain. Ibrahima and Moktar sang and recited the poetry that is the wine of Moorish culture, filled with its past and present and at the tip of every man's tongue. Much later, Moktar and Ibrahima and the others staggered off into the night to sleep in the village. We could hear their voices for a long time, coming back from the gorge. I only woke once in the night, when a wind picked up to stir the palm trees, rubbing and rustling their dark heads together and creaking their long slim trunks.

The next day, after breakfasting on the cold remains of the meat, we set off back to Atar. In Tergit we crossed a convoy of huge overland luxury vehicles with tinted glass and two-way radios, an expedition from the American Embassy. The sight of it brought me briefly back from the beautiful, harsh lands I was in to contemplation of a more ordinary, functional existence. We took a fast, direct route back to Atar and had two punctures a mile short of the town. Moktar dropped Jean and me at Mohammed's restaurant. We shook hands with Ibrahima and all our companions.

'You see, I still have my ears intact,' Moktar said, pulling one of them as he drove off.

9

Old Chinguetti

Chinguetti was an old desert town some hundred-and-twenty kilometres due west of Atar, on the edge of the El Mreyye, one of the most harsh and waterless deserts of the western Sahara. The same day that Jean set off for Nouadhibou to resume his work, I found a Landrover bound for Chinguetti.

The journey was long and monotonous across a rocky plain scourged by a bitter wind heavily laden with dust and sand. At one time two men appeared out of the swirling greyness and flagged us down. They were all turbans and eagle noses and they peered long and hard through the Landrover window at the European. Then they were off again into the wind.

The old town of Chinguetti, when we suddenly came across it, was just a strip of stone houses across a large *oued* or dry river bed. And that strip of houses was under siege: in the midst of a ferocious storm, the entire surface of the earth was loose and shifting. Regiments of sand dunes marched off to the east and to the west, and directly behind the town the sand built up like huge waves about to break. The town felt ancient. What else could explain this small 'port', sitting on the edge of a great desert sea, so firmly anchored against the blind tempest of the elements?

And indeed Chinguetti was an ancient town, one of a string of old caravan towns throughout the Sahara, the most renowned of which is Timbuktou. Since the early days of civilisation there has been a trans-Sahara trade, merchants from the Maghreb in the north of Africa meeting the peoples of the lands south of the Sahara. In exchange for fine cloth, glass beads, copperware, guns and paper, the merchants received ivory, kola nuts, ostrich feathers and slaves, whose blood, over the centuries, merged with their own. The most significant trade, though, was that of salt for gold. West Africa was rich in gold, panned from rivers and dug from shallow mines, but it had none of the salt which black Africans so craved. The Maghrebian merchants obligingly mined salt in the depths of the Sahara, where it was plentiful, and transported it south, at one time exchanging it for equal weights in gold. Kingdoms and empires in the Sudan grew up from this trade, and from the knowledge and culture of a wider world that came with it: new concepts of law and government and learning, new

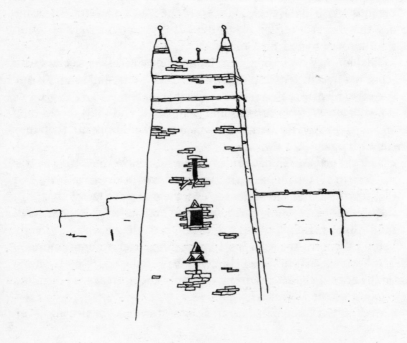

skills and words for languages and, most importantly, a new religion, Islam.

The camel caravans used the towns on the trading routes to water and provision themselves and they grew into important markets, with many different peoples drawn there to settle. They became affluent and cosmopolitan, with a rich, varied culture. Chinguetti became a centre of Islamic learning and in time it was recognised as one of the seven holy cities of Islam, a mustering point from which pilgrims set out on the yearly *hadj* to Mecca; on one particular day it was recorded that a caravan of 52,000 camels had set out from there on the *hadj*. For a time the whole of the western Sahara was known as the land of 'Shingit', named after the pilgrims of Chinguetti.

I made a friend on my first day in town, a radio mender called Isslemou. His boutique was in the small, modern part of town across the *oued* from the old town. In the morning I had found myself wandering self-consciously round this area, being followed by many sets of eyes wherever I went. Round and round I walked, feeling more and more idiotic as the town watched me pass by again and again. Then Isslemou popped his head out of his boutique and invited me in for tea. What a relief! I bolted in, away from all those eyes.

The shop looked as if someone had just lobbed in a hand grenade. It was chaos. The wooden counter was on its side diagonally across half the room. The tall metal shelving that ran up the back wall had broken away at one end and hung forwards precariously, the shelves spilling a mass of what must have been radio components to the floor, where they met the debris of other electrical and mechanical paraphernalia, broken, snapped, burnt, shattered and scattered at random, gradually forming a small hill in one corner.

Isslemou directed me behind the counter where I found a circle of men squatting on the floor, brewing tea. They were an assorted bunch, mostly old but varying in shade from those who were almost white to those who were black and those who had gone blue from indigo turbans. One of them, an ancient, scraggy old man, had on a pair of glasses, cracked and strapped to his face by a system of wires; the lenses were so scratched that from my side I could barely see his eyes. Another of them, the darkest of blacks, looked as if he was carved from stone, so still and serenely did he sit, his two massive arms folded in front of him like a Buddha. He sat making the tea, staring at the pot as though in a trance. Everybody was scruffy and dirty, *bobos* stained and turbans partially unravelled and hanging in big loops below chins. I shook hands all round and they moved over to make space for me.

Isslemou sat down against the wall and, picking up a radio, went back to work. He had an intelligent, easy-go-lucky face, a halo of amazingly disorganised hair and a *bobo* that had once in its life been white. There was a good atmosphere in his shop, a sort of continuous tea-break mood. I ended up spending a lot of time there. Everybody who came in was naturally inquisitive and asked me all the usual questions. I gave my, by now, routine answers, but other than that I found I was easily accepted into the run of things. The men would teach me some Hassaniyya and I would tell them odd things about my country, which greatly amused them.

There were long conversations that went on in the shop, that rambled and rose and fell like the course of a long river to the sea. I did not understand them, so Isslemou would explain parts to me.

'You see, this man here,' he would say, indicating one of our circle, 'has five sheep, and because his brother-in-law is in debt to one of the *patrons* in town and because this man sometimes works for the *patron*, transporting rocks on his donkey for the construction of a new house the *patron* is building, the *patron* says that he should not pay this man unless he gives him two of his sheep in payment for his brother-in-law's debt. This other man here is of the opinion that this man ought not to be responsible for his brother-in-law's debts. This man here says that he should be but that the *patron* ought to arrange the fetching of the two sheep that are sixteen kilometres away in the desert, and this man over here says that he should be responsible for his brother-in-law's debts and because of the delay in payment he should be the one to go and look for the sheep.'

It was not always easy to follow Isslemou's explanations, especially as he continually interrupted himself by joining in the increasingly labyrinthine conversation. His pronouncements were listened to attentively, because Isslemou was respected for being very sensible in matters of this sort.

Each morning I would go and drink tea in his shop. It was a focal point of the market area and Isslemou seemed to be an important man in the mechanics of town life. He did not just mend radios, he was a man who *did* things for people, so they were continually popping in to ask favours.

'You know the adjutant up at the army barracks?' a man might say. 'Can you ask him to reserve me a place in the army truck going to Atar tomorrow?'

Or, 'My brother needs two fine sheep for his forthcoming marriage. Can you see if you can find two cheap ones for me, Isslemou?'

Isslemou knew everybody and everybody knew and, at some time or another, needed Isslemou. At midday he would close his shop and go round town on his errands, popping into boutiques to see if they needed any more cooking oil – he had heard that there was a spare drum of it arriving in the Landrover from Atar that evening – or nipping into the police posts for quick conversations, generally making himself useful and indispensable to the life of the town.

Isslemou had two wives. They lived at opposite ends of the town from each other. His first wife knew about the second wife, but the second did not know about the first, and thought that she herself was the first. He took me to meet them one day. His first wife lived at the far end of the old town in an area of devastation and abandonment. Many of the houses were tall and well constructed, with immensely thick walls, courtyards and deep, dark rooms as cool as larders. They had once been the abodes of a sophisticated people and were built like forts to keep out enemies and the elements. Many of them were half-buried under sand dunes now and there were only occasional pockets of humanity, children who ran away shouting, 'Nasrani, Nasrani,' and women pounding grain.

We entered his courtyard, really just an area of sand surrounded by the shells of broken homes. His wife was sitting on the ground cradling a naked child who wailed feebly. She did not look happy and told Isslemou that the child was ill. He did not pay much attention to her and we went into a room in one of the old rock-built houses, empty but for a mat and some pieces of clothing stuffed into the holes in the walls. Isslemou shouted for his wife to bring us some tea and peanuts. She did so without speaking and as soon as the tea was finished we left.

'Ah, she is a bad woman, that,' said Isslemou, when we were outside. 'She does not know how to treat a guest properly and always she is complaining of something. I think I will divorce her soon, she only troubles me.'

His other wife lived in a *tegit* on a sand dune on the fringes of the town. She was younger and happier than the first and she invited us into her home with a warm smile. Stooping down, I found myself in a nest of blankets and colourful mats with two green tin trunks at one end. She mixed a bowl of milk powder for us and gave Isslemou the implements to make tea.

'Please, please, relax, lie down, feel at home,' Isslemou said. 'This is a good house.'

So I lay back and while they talked together I watched her do what every family woman in Mauritania has to do every day: make the couscous, the staple diet of the desert. She sat by the small door, through which nothing could be seen but a wall of sand. Drops of water were added to millet powder which was rubbed on a wicker platter until tiny lumps formed; these were shaken into a bowl to dry before they were steamed for eating. It was a long process and she worked slowly and methodically, rubbing and shaking, rubbing and shaking, to the light coming through the door. It was calming and mesmeric watching her work and soon I had to sit up so as not to doze off. As it became dark we got up to go. Before we left, the girl dug in one of her green trunks and pulled out a string of beads, a present from her to my wife, she told me. I took it, even though I had no wife.

Outside it was almost night, that brief spell of time between dusk and full night when the world seems to hold its breath and all around is momentarily settled and still and indefinable. The sand dunes looked slightly luminous as if they were releasing some of the energy and sunlight that had poured down on them all day. As we walked back I asked Isslemou to explain to me a bit about all the different types of people to be found in Chinguetti. He laughed and went on to confuse me even more in this complex matter of ancestry and colour.

'Ha, ha,' he chuckled, 'so you are confused. You see, sometimes a black Moor can be a noble black Moor, sometimes he can be a white Moor. Sometimes he is a servant, sometimes a slave. It depends on his parenthood. And a white Moor can sometimes be inferior to a black Moor, or he can be a noble white Moor or he can be a subservient white Moor. We are all Moors, but we are all different colours, are we not? But then the colour of someone has little to do with whether he is noble or not, or a white Moor or not. You see, there are warriors who are Berbers and Berbers who are *marabouts*. And there are Arabs who are warriors and *marabouts* who call themselves Arabs but who are in fact Berbers. There are even men who are neither, but black Africans who call themselves Arab. Do you see?'

Well, I did not exactly see but I said, 'I thought slavery had been abolished in Mauritania. How can someone be a slave then?'

'A man bought a slave and he has not sold him so he is still his slave,' said Isslemou, simply. At that moment we were passing two women carrying baskets on their heads. Isslemou grabbed one of them by the arm and said, 'Look, here is an Abid, a slave, you see.'

The girl pulled her arm free and said something to him that did not sound like the words of a slave, but Isslemou only laughed.

Before going to Isslemou's shop to have tea every morning I would go for a long walk. Sometimes I would just walk out behind the town into the sand dunes. I would stroll about them for a while, marvelling at their razor-edged curves and their wind-rippled slopes. I would imagine to myself what it would be like just to keep walking, to walk far into the sand sea to discover a whole treasure chest of newly shaped dunes as virgin and untouched as the surface of the moon. One morning I found a man digging up stones in one of the patches of gravel that sometimes lay between the dunes. This was where the rust-coloured stone of Chinguetti's buildings came from. The man dug the sand away from small boulders, then levered them up with an iron rod to be cracked like eggs with a big hammer, revealing their pale insides for the first time since their birth.

Nearer the town I came across a group of men digging out a small house that was nearly submerged in sand. They put the sand in sacks and dragged them a short distance away, emptying it out to be blown on to the next house. The old man directing the operation came over to me and, digging in his *bobo* pocket, solemnly produced a handkerchief. Unravelling it in his hand, he showed me ten or twelve arrowheads made from chips of stone. They dated back to the neolithic hunters who had inhabited the Sahara before it was a desert, when it was a green savannah supporting game herds and even elephant and rhinoceros. These arrowheads were very common, he told me, the local people often finding them where they had been uncovered by a shifting sand dune. Some of them were of very pretty design and colour and I felt tempted when he asked me if I wanted to buy any.

Often, as I was wandering in the plains round the town, small groups of children, the sons and daughters of local herdsmen, would see me from afar and, recognising that I was European, would steer a course to meet my particular trajectory; then, when we met, they would follow me silently. When I spoke to them they would giggle to each other shyly and hang back a bit, as if I was dangerous, but when we came to a sand dune they would somersault and cartwheel down its long steep sides for me. Later, they would ask the inevitable question that all children in Mauritania ask Europeans.

'*Cadeaux, bonbons?*'

And if I had any in my pocket I would hand them over and so confirm their belief that Europeans are a natural and infallible source of sweets.

In its heyday, Chinguetti had been rich in palm groves. Most of the palms had died in ancient droughts and nowadays there were only a few, thin *palmeries* on the banks of the *oued*. Each one was divided into separate enclosures by walls of reeds and each enclosure had a well in it.

I would often sit and watch someone watering his enclosure from the well. Some people concentrated on growing vegetables and had perhaps fifteen or twenty small plots of carrots and onions and tomatoes. But not many of them did this; vegetables were not regarded as serious food by the Moors. They liked meat and starch and would only chuck a carrot in the pot now and again as an afterthought. One man that I sometimes watched had about fifty date palms with plots of millet and barley beneath them. The wells were operated by a pivoted balance called a *shelah*, a long strip of palm trunk weighted at one end by rocks strapped on by camel hide, and at the other a rope and a rubber bucket. The wells were deep and getting deeper each year as the water table fell, due to the lack of good rains. Each morning this man would spend two or three hours

pulling the rope down, lowering the bucket and raising the stones at the far end of the *shelah*; when the bucket was full the *shelah* was equally balanced and so the bucket was easier to pull up. He would stand stripped to the waist with a foot either side of the well, sweat streaming down him as he worked with fast, coarse hands on the rope. Each day he would lift maybe a hundred buckets of water to fill a small pond in front of the well. When this was full he would open sluices at its side and the water would flow to his palm trees and plots of millet and barley through a system of small channels. He used to complain that the work he put in was not worth the gains:

the Aid-donated grain in the boutiques was very cheap, making it hardly worth all this work each day.

'If only I had a pump,' he said to me, or, 'If only the rains would be what they used to be.'

And so I would pass my mornings, talking to and watching the acquaintances I made: the stone quarrier, the palm grove workers and a stone mason who was building a new house. These people were always friendly and did not mind me watching them at work. Later, Isslemou would greet me at the door to his shop as if I had not seen him for days and then go back to his work. He was a slapdash but clever worker. Nothing could confound him. From his huge stock of junk he utilised the most unlikely things in the most ingenious ways. He worked on the floor in the dust and sand, talking continually as he worked, sipping tea, arguing with the customers who came in, his hands working quite independently of his eyes or concentration. Someone brought in a cassette jammed solid with sand and dust. The tape had snapped but it was not a thing to be thrown away and abandoned. No, he simply left the cassette in a glass of soapy water overnight, in the morning shook it dry and then, taking the two broken ends of the tape in a pair of pliers, applied a hot coal from the brazier so that they melted together. He put the cassette into a machine and it worked perfectly.

I asked Isslemou if he knew anybody who could cut my hair. He took me to one of the local smithies. Cross-legged on the floor of his house, the smith sat surrounded by the bits and pieces of his trade: scrap metal, an anvil and rudimentary tools. His fire was not lit, he said, because he had very little work. In fact, he told us, it was a good week if he had to light his fire twice – there were so few people in town these days. It was only people like Isslemou who managed to make a living.

'You see, everybody has a radio,' he said.

Isslemou wanted his mop of hair cut too, so he went first. A white cape was thrown professionally around him, his head sticking out of the top like a coconut in a coconut-shy. With scissors the size of sheep shears, the smith literally sheared Isslemou, starting on one side of his head and working to the other, removing the entire crop. Large clumps of hair fell to the ground and a couple of sheep that had been standing at the door watching us started chewing them. When the operation was finished Isslemou was as bald as a convict. He patted his head vainly and asked me if it looked all right.

'Yes, it looks fine,' I told him, not caring to mention the odd trickle of blood where he had been snipped. I decided not to have my hair cut just then after all.

I stayed eight days in Chinguetti; eight gentle, idle days. I was lodging in a place calling itself the 'Maison de bien être'. It belonged to a man called Mohammed, a *sharif*, a Muslim leader and a descendant of Mohammed, the prophet. He was a man of extreme politeness and dignity. He was also a shrewd man and one of the richest in town. There was no commerce to speak of now, so he had other projects in hand in order to remain rich; this he had to do because he had a big family and many dependants and servants to feed. He had built a bakery, the only one in town, and he had built the 'Maison de bien être', a kind of rest house for travellers and tourists. There were a few of them who came to Chinguetti these days, mostly people interested in history.

The 'Maison de bien être' was freshly whitewashed and hidden behind a tall wall. There were two Beduin tents filled with expensive carpets and cushions, a small, modern kitchen and a long, windowless room adjoining the house where Mohammed lived with his family.

'There is no charge for staying here,' Mohammed informed me the evening I arrived. 'It is a tradition in this town to lodge a guest for as long as he wishes to stay, even if it is a year or two years or ten years. And never will the guest be asked to pay. He will not be asked for so much as a penny. But of course,' he continued, in a cordial tone of voice and with a smile on his face, 'when a guest comes to leave, if he is happy with the hospitality he has received, he may wish to give a small present to his host. It is the customary thing to do, you know.'

I settled in very comfortably. I would pass each evening and night on my own, sleeping in the long windowless room beside the Beduin

106

tents. One of Mohammed's sons would bring me a dish of couscous, then I would be left with the silence of the desert that lay all around and the darkness of the long room flickering to my candle, shadows bounding about like demons. I never felt lonely. The dark, empty nights drew poems and fantastic thoughts from me and when I slept I slipped into the void with an ease I had never known, untroubled even by dreams. In the mornings Mohammed would wake me.

'Come, come, the day is here,' he would call into the room, letting a bright strip of it penetrate to where I lay. 'Ah, you Europeans like your beds too much. Come, get up.'

As I sat breakfasting on some of the hot French bread from his bakery, I would watch Mohammed ordering his servants in the watering of the few plots of vegetables and wheat he was growing in front of the tents. He would stand there in his immaculate white *bobo*, stiff as a board, hands clasped behind his back. He would never use his hands, which were fine and delicate, for anything: when he wanted to indicate something he would point with his foot.

'No, no. Put more water there,' he would point. 'Block that channel there and divert the water that way, there, can't you see?'

The couple of young men who did this work for him were very patient. Sometimes, when they had been scolded by Mohammed and I had been a witness to it, they would come up to me later and say, 'Mohammed is a good man, he is a fair and just man. He is an honest man, he is our *patron*, our father, a truly good and generous man.'

Towards the end of my stay in Chinguetti I decided that I would go by camel to the Tagant province in the south. Isslemou told me there were very few camels in Chinguetti, so it was not going to be easy to find one. The first step, he said, was to spread the word that I was looking for a camel and a guide. I was viewed with general but polite scepticism. 'Can you eat millet? . . . Can you eat with your hands? . . . Will you be able to sleep outside?' people would ask me. At last someone told us to try two men who had recently acquired some camels.

At this time there were local elections going on throughout

107

Mauritania. A man from Nouakchott had been sent to Chinguetti to observe the voting and to give patriotic speeches. Isslemou and I found the first camelman listening to one of these. A rostrum had been erected in the *oued*, upon which sat the town dignitaries and army officers and the man from Nouakchott, a large crowd on the ground in front of them. The man from Nouakchott had just finished his speech. He was smooth and city-looking and wore dark, drooping sunglasses. An older man, with a thick black beard and a huge pile of high-quality turban, rose from the crowd. He gave a short, fierce speech about voting with morality and honesty and then sat down abruptly, looking angry. The crowd loved him and clapped and cheered, so again he rose up and bellowed at the rostrum where the Nouakchott man sat, impassive and serious behind his sunglasses.

When the older man sat down again the meeting broke up. The sun had just sunk across the *oued* and the bubbling crowd drifted off. The man who had given the last speech was the one we were looking for. We approached him and in a long speech Isslemou told him who I was and what I wanted. He seemed totally uninterested, merely replying to Isslemou that he would not rent his camel to a European for any amount of money. He looked at me with something like contempt and, taking advantage of the crowd that had now gathered round, gave another of his short, fierce speeches, this time I fear with myself as the subject. But the crowd was in a light and jolly mood after the excitement of the oratory; people shook my hand and pelted me with questions about my proposed camel trip, and when Isslemou and I eventually managed to extricate ourselves they remained where they were, discussing the price they thought I ought to pay.

We did not have much more success with the next man we tried. Again Isslemou gave his speech, going to great lengths to elaborate on my character and drawing a vivid picture of my crossing the desert. The man stood there all the while, listening patiently, but when Isslemou eventually came to my price he simply turned his back and walked off without a word.

'Don't be dispirited,' Isslemou told me. 'With patience, things always turn up.'

In the next couple of days while I was waiting, a group of Italian tourists came to the 'Maison de bien être'. They were amazed when I told them I had known about their coming two days previously. It was true. Isslemou had told me that a party of six Italians, two of them women, travelling in two Landrovers, one of which was having engine problems, would be arriving in Chinguetti today from another old desert town called Ouadane, and that they would be staying for only one night.

'But we did not even know for sure ourselves that we were coming to Chinguetti two days ago!' said the Italians.

There is a very efficient bush telegraph service in the desert. There are so few people and so few meeting points that when anything of the remotest interest happens, news spreads quickly. Traditionally, one of the first things desert people do on meeting each other is to exchange information: which camel herds have gone where; how the pastures are in a certain place; which of the local vehicles that run about the desert is running where, for what reasons, for how long; who has died recently or who is ill; how much a goat is selling for in the north; almost anything, down to the upturning of a particular stone in a particular piece of desert. Naturally, the touring of a group of Italians was not something that would pass unnoticed and their movements could be predicted on the basis of the various facts that came along with the news of their existence. Of course the Italians would come to Chinguetti, even if they had not been aware of it themselves, but only after going to Ouadane. They had visited a certain oasis from which they either had to return to Atar or continue to Ouadane. The latter was the more obvious course because they were historians; and then on leaving Ouadane, they would either have to return to the oasis, which was unlikely, or come on to Chinguetti. As everybody knew they were in a hurry, they could only spend one day in Ouadane, which in turn meant that they would arrive here today and then have to be off tomorrow, because that left only two days to return to Nouakchott where they had a flight booked back

109

to Italy. There was almost a welcoming party waiting for their arrival.

The passing of news is an important part of desert life, so well refined that there is in fact little more privacy in the empty vastness than there is in a small village. Without this, how could people know where the grazing was good and whether some other camels were already there? How could you know which wells had water and which had none? It could be fatal to end up at a dry well with a thirsty herd of camels or goats. And how would you know where there were good supplies of grain at a price you could afford? It was during all those many hours sitting over cups of tea that the sum of a person's knowledge grew until he had a fine and constantly updated picture of the land about him, upon which he depended for his survival.

The Italians told me they were not very impressed with Mauritania. They had been trekking round the desert for a month now and were tired and dirty. They had come to see the ancient things of Mauritania but had discovered that most of them were neglected or buried deep beneath the sand dunes. Isslemou told me when they had left that he thought it very strange that the four Italian men should have to share only two women.

'Why did they not bring one each?' he asked.

Two days later Isslemou's efforts to find me a camel and a guide bore fruit. A man who introduced himself as Ahmed of Chinguetti said he had heard in his camp twenty kilometres away that I was looking for a camel to go to the Tagant. He was an oldish man who wore a simple, coarse tunic tied about his middle with a piece of rope, like a monk. His face was grizzled with white stubble, his underlip protruded and quivered whenever he was confused or angry, and the hand he offered me to shake was so hard and calloused it was like grabbing a piece of wood.

The day before we left Isslemou took me off to get my shoes mended; the soles were falling off. He took me to a family who lived, like Isslemou's first wife, in the ruins of one of the old houses. They were very poor people. The grandmother, who looked so old and fragile that a puff of wind might blow her away, stripped threads of leather from a camel hide for her daughter to stitch up my soles.

In the daughter's lap was a small boy with deep, sad eyes and a runny nose. Between the two women, lying on a sack amidst rubble and scraps, was the daughter's husband. He was blind. His eyes were grey sockets of skin but he had the gentle, compassionate face of the very devout. The woman and the child had terrible hacking coughs and spat globs of phlegm at the crumbling wall which the woman wiped off with the corner of her shawl. Flies crawled over everything, into everyone's eyes, noses and mouths, sucking up the salty moisture. A young girl sat by her father, holding his hand and staring at me, making no attempt to wave off the clusters of flies hanging at her eyes. Everything about the room and the people in it reeked of disease, but they were a kind, friendly family. They made me tea and shared pieces of bread with me and made jokes about my shoes so that we could laugh together. The husband, being blind, could do nothing but sit all day while his wife and her mother stitched and wove leather mats and cushions to earn enough for them to eat. Chinguetti had fallen on sad days, I thought to myself. No longer are the houses filled with fat merchants and their fat servants.

That night I was woken by a pattering sound on the tin roof of my long room. When I opened the door to look outside I saw fat drops of rain, landing on the ground in little explosions of dust. The air smelled as it does after a downpour on summer city pavements but next morning there was no indication that it had ever rained.

I left Chinguetti that evening after a day of buying provisions and organisation. I said goodbye to Mohammed and negotiated the present I should leave him for the hospitality he had given me. Isslemou gave me a list of useful Hassaniyya words that I might need in my travels, and I gave him a present of some money. The evening was one of the clearest I had so far had in Chinguetti. Just by the 'Maison de bien être' a wedding circle had formed in the oued. The people were dressed in their best bright colours. In the rays of the evening sun they looked like a garland of flowers as they sang and clapped in time to a drum beat. I left to the sounds of celebration, to the sounds of optimism for the continued existence of the old town of Chinguetti, passing, with Ahmed leading the camel, into the dunes behind the town. Now and again I caught a glimpse of it as we ascended a dune, but before long it was gone and there was just myself, Ahmed, the camel and miles of stretching golden sand.

10

A long walk

I have often wondered what it is about deserts that makes them so attractive, so compelling, at least to some people. They are not attractive places in the ordinary sense of the word, and they are certainly not comfortable. Their landscapes are often an infinity of monotony swept over by sand-laced winds and shimmering with an intensity of heat that quite excludes the possibility of enjoyment. They have none of the obvious diversity and colour of tropical places and none of their profusion and abundance: in the desert one is resigned to a spartan life. Yet there are people so bitten by the desert that they cannot have enough of it, must always return to it, sometimes even compelled on and on by a force that may bring them close to death. Is this what they seek – death? Or a life spent in a place where death is readily meted out? Is the desert, then, the last escape, or is it in fact quite the opposite, a place where one is forced into terms with oneself and one's fellow men, a place where all is revealed because in the desert you can hide nothing?

I was now committed to a three-hundred kilometre or so walk in the desert. I was going to a town called Rachid in the province of Tagant. I had a camel that carried my bag, a sack of food supplies and two *guerbas*, or goatskin water carriers. The *guerbas* dripped water at an alarming rate because they were porous, but in fact this allowed the water to keep reasonably cool by evaporation. I had a black turban to wrap around my head and face to keep the heat and dust a little at bay. Ahmed, my guide, spoke no word of French and I had only the very basics in Hassaniyya.

Ahmed led the camel by a long rope attached to a ring in one of its nostrils. For much of the time he walked in bare feet, carrying a small cutting axe and a stick that he held levelled along his shoulders, his arms draped over either end like a scarecrow's. I followed behind in their tracks and that was the order of march for the next eight days. We walked fast, we rarely spoke and we stopped only once each day, some time around noon. I shall not readily forget the view I came to know so well, of the back of the camel swaying from side to side as he plodded methodically forwards, the pile of gear on his back shifting and creaking with each step; and Ahmed, striding with a straight back and level shoulders as though on a catwalk, into one vast landscape after another.

It was a hard eight days, perhaps the hardest I had experienced in my, up till then, not very hard life. We passed through a land that was dead, or at least dying; a land laid to waste after the goats and the villagers' axes and the droughts had done their work, virtually abandoned, a no-man's-land.

For the first day we were in the large sand sea that stretched away behind Chinguetti, the sand sea I had so often imagined walking into. And I was not disappointed. There was nothing but sand dunes; sand dunes of every imaginable and curious design, some as high as small mountains with no footprint or rock or even a stone to blemish their smooth sides. The only sign of man was the neolithic arrowheads, of which I found one and Ahmed two.

The first night set the pattern for those that followed. Shortly before dusk, finding a spot preferably shielded from the wind, such as behind a sand dune, and if possible near a source of wood like a dead tree, we would make camp. The camel, to whom I gave the not very original name of Jemel, this being the Arabic for camel, would be unloaded by Ahmed. Couched, he would gurgle and snarl and snap as Ahmed loosened the ropes tied firmly round him. Once free of his burden, he would stagger up, shake himself and stand still for a while, viewing the world down his long nose. Then he would make off to the surrounding desert where he would spend the night browsing, Ahmed having hobbled him so that he could not wander too far. Ahmed would then spread a blanket on the ground and set about collecting wood for a fire. I would flop down on to the blanket, as by then I was generally in a state of extreme exhaustion and thirst. It took all my concentrated effort to achieve one objective: to sit patiently while Ahmed went about his chores and not to scream, 'Water, water. Give me water.'

Once Ahmed had a small fire going he would make some tea; the hot, sweet essence would explode in my mouth and do more for my thirst than a gallon of water. Once this was finished and Ahmed had washed the teapot and glasses, carefully drinking the water he cleaned them with, he would set another pot of water on the fire to boil. Our main supply of food was millet powder, not for couscous but for a thick, dry porridge to which Ahmed added large amounts of cooking oil. We then washed our hands, Ahmed thanked God for the food, and we ate. Ahmed could eat vast amounts of this food but as the days went by I had more and more difficulty in digesting it; the cooking oil became a deep and dire enemy. By the time the meal was over it would be well and truly dark, so we would lie down side by side on the blanket and go to sleep.

The evenings were mostly silent, since we could not say much to each other, but we made up for it by smiling at each other a lot. Ahmed was a silent man, anyway. He had about himself the air of a camel: distant, dignified, well poised, and looking as if he was permanently mildly suffering but had resigned himself to this fate. He was also a devout Muslim, said his prayers regularly and thanked God for all that befell him in life, good or bad. I had implicit trust in his quiet, gentle manner and felt that he would go through thick and thin for his companion if he thought that was the right thing to do.

The first night was cold and moonless and before going to sleep I lay a while looking up at the stars. How dull and plain were the night skies I had admired in the past. What I saw that night was like seeing three-dimensionally for the first time, like seeing colour after a lifetime of black-and-white. The stars and space were not just something above me: lying on the side of a sand dune on the face of a dark, bare planet, I was amongst the stars, I was in space. It fell all about me, the very air in front of my nose was space, the same inky space that towered above me; a deep, infinite well that one minute made me want to cling to the earth so as not to be spun away into it, and the next pressed down, pinning me like an insect to the barrenness that lay all about me. And instead of there being just stars – stationary, obvious points of light – the sky was ablaze with motion and strange happenings. There were shooting stars that sailed on steady courses across my entire vision; there were meteorites flashing every few minutes into the earth's atmosphere; there were points of light that came and went as some unknown cloud of solar gas moved in front of them; and there were inexplicable flashes of light, like sheet lightning. If I looked at the black spaces between the billions of stars and stared hard for a while and blinked a little, suddenly the blank space was filled with another million stars as tiny and elusive as grains of dust. The weight of all these stars pressed down upon me with a terrible indifference. It was almost intimidating. There was nowhere to hide from all this universe that put all my efforts, my very being, into tiny, ridiculous perspective. There was nowhere in this desert to escape from a bigger reality. I became acutely aware of the vulnerability of my small body of bones and desperately pumping blood. I was almost scared for a while – I was in the desert and had to face this exposure for the next eight days. I pulled my sleeping bag over my head and found comfort in its familiar texture, and slept.

The land we walked in for the first few days was a series of large plains, each one of which took six or seven hours to cross and each ending in a low escarpment that stepped up to the next one like a giant staircase. Sometimes the plains were dotted with small, solitary sand dunes identical in shape with their round, rippled backs to the wind, which skimmed loose sand up the surface to let it fall down the sharp, curved slope of the leeward side of the dune, so gradually inching it forwards. In other places the dunes would be held up by some obstacle, a gully or a hill or even something as small as a bush or rock. Immobilised, they soon grew in size. Others would join them and so a small sand sea would develop, but mostly the plains were pebbly and rocky, gently undulating, here and there breaking up into gullies and small *oueds*. At one place I found a single slab of rock about one kilometre across, as flat and smooth as slate. It was only when one climbed one of the escarpments and turned round that one gained an impression of the land as a whole. Then you could see great distances, the gentle falling-away of the plain to large sand seas in the east and west that shimmered in the heat haze, lakes of mirage water perhaps lying at their feet. Sometimes there would be low hills on the horizon to help us steer a new course; some areas we came to would be strewn with the limbs of small, dead, gnarled trees.

As we walked along I noticed that Ahmed and Jemel were continually communicating with each other. Camels are a particularly intelligent breed of animal; slow, methodical, even plodding, perhaps, but entirely independent and although domesticated, most certainly not subservient, though they will sometimes tolerate humans behaving as if they are in control. When the load on Jemel's back went off-balance, as it often did, and slipped to one side, threatening to fall off, Jemel would inform Ahmed, walking ahead of him, with a few grunts. If the load was sitting properly but rubbing in some place, Ahmed would quickly realise the problem because Jemel would stamp his feet and roll his eyes. But of much more interest to me as I walked along behind them was the communication that seemed to go on for no other reason than to reassure each other of their continued existence.

Jemel, like all camels, had the habit of chewing the cud. Camels have a complex and versatile internal system that can digest nearly anything and store huge amounts of water. This internal arrangement gurgles and burps continually, like a hot water system, the end product being a regurgitated green slime. Jemel used this slime to make a gurgling noise in his throat. He was very versatile at this and could quite clearly communicate anger, scorn, pleasure, mild annoyance or contentment. In response Ahmed clicked his tongue and umph-ed and aargh-ed.

Whenever we passed a clump of dried grass Ahmed would bend down to pull it up and feed it to Jemel. Jemel, however, did not always want to eat and so would spit it out. What Jemel did not and of course could not know was that we were on a long walk in a barren desert, consequently that there would be few, if any, opportunities for good grazing for eight days – so he had better make the most of any clump of grass we came across, no matter how dry and unappetising it might be. So Ahmed would pick the clump of grass up again and forcibly stuff it back between Jemel's teeth. Jemel would then hold it for a while doing nothing, but looking rather foolish. When Ahmed once again had his back turned, Jemel would let it drop to the ground for a second time, but would make the mistake of giving his triumphant gurgle. This would alert Ahmed, who would casually pick up the clump of grass again and put it back between Jemel's teeth. The battle of wills would continue until usually Ahmed won. Then Jemel would walk along for a while, chewing, and looking from side to side as if nothing had been lost.

Jemel was not a handsome beast. In many places his hair was worn down to his hide, like a pair of old shoes. He had ticks all over his knobbly legs, and his head was heavy and square, with two small, shredded ears that twitched back and forth like a mouse's. But he was big and strong and no more evil-tempered than any other camel and, as all his kind seem to, he knew that it was the humans who depended upon him rather than the other way round.

For the first day and a half we did not see any people. Not that there was no life around us. We often saw harriers spiralling high above on air thermals and there were many crows that hopped about amongst the rocks, squawking and stabbing at black beetles. There were also many types of lizard, some quite large, which scrabbled away at our approach. The sand was a veritable dictionary of insect tracks woven into haphazard and seemingly very roundabout patterns.

118

At one time we startled a desert fox digging a hole in the side of a sand dune. For a few seconds he stood stock-still, his big, woolly bat ears that are so finely designed to cool his circulating blood, twitching in our direction. Then he was off, dashing over the dune out of sight. One night, when we were eating supper, we were invaded by lots of sandy-coloured mice. They were quite unafraid of us and scampered over our legs, grabbing bits of fallen food until they became a nuisance. Ahmed put a brutal stop to their play by whacking them with one of his sandals. Then we had three dead mice lying at our feet.

By the third day we started coming across the occasional person. The first of these appeared one afternoon. I had been trudging in the tracks of Jemel as usual, completely lost in some deep thoughts and quite confident that on the vast open plain we were the only living things, when suddenly there was a man beside me. It gave me quite a jolt. He was on his way to Chinguetti from Aen Savra, he said, the only village between Chinguetti and Rachid, where we were headed. We stopped with him for a while to brew some tea, crouching behind a small bush for protection against the fierce wind. This man had nothing with him but a richly decorated walking stick, his pipe and a tobacco pouch. Soon another man appeared, a small dot rushing from a short horizon, who turned out to be very old and partially blind. Again, he had nothing with him but a walking stick. They drank our tea with us but would accept no water or food. They were travelling light and fast and presumably preferred to wait until the end of their journey before slaking their thirst and hunger. This

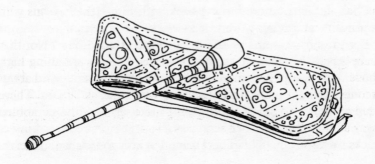

was obviously no expedition for them, merely a two- or three-day jaunt from one village to the next. Quite how the old man could see his way I could not guess, but then in the old days some of the best desert guides for caravans and military expeditions had been blind. They found their way with their other senses; the smell of the wind, the texture of the sand, sounds and other devices, like those of migratory birds, that we of the modern world have yet to understand.

A day later a man with three white camels overtook us. One of the camels was a mother, another a young, elegant female and the third a baby, all legs, tall and spindly like a daddy-long-legs. It had long, delicate eyelashes and trotted after its mother, getting left behind now and again. The man was vigorous and handsome, as tough and well-finished as tempered steel. He ran and walked alternately, herding the camels before him, shoo-ing them this way and that on a zigzagging course that ran an eventually true line to the south. He said a few words to Ahmed as he passed but did not stop, running off to the horizon like a long-distance runner. I felt leaden and doltish by comparison, for by the end of the day I had to force my legs every step of the way and my head was thick and dull after the hours of exposure to the bludgeoning glare and heat of the sun and the continual roar of the wind.

As so the days passed. The weather, which had at first been cold, even well into the morning, warmed up and each day became harder for me to bear. Ahmed would wake me each morning in the early pre-dawn hours by fumbling with the fire and our sack of supplies. Then he would be off to find Jemel. Sometimes it would be as much as half an hour before he was back with him, Jemel gurgling his complaint at having to return to work. At midday every day we stopped and ate some of the dried bread Ahmed had brought to supplement the millet, mixed with water, or sometimes Ahmed would make kisera, a millet cake baked in the hot sand and ashes below a fire. It would be burnt and coated with sand and I could never determine why Ahmed would then mash it up with the same water he had just washed it with.

As I walked I thought. There was often little to look at and nothing

120

to do but walk, so I would let my mind wander on long, rambling daydreams. On one occasion we were walking across a sandy plain, following the line of a row of low hills to the east of us, when I saw coming towards us a small expedition similar to our own: two men and a camel. As they drew nearer I was surprised to see that the man mounted on the camel was another European. He was dressed in a typical office suit, soiled and crumpled as if he had been living in it for several days, topped off by a badly adjusted turban. His face was beetroot red and he was wearing a pair of glasses which were all steamed up. He stopped a little short of us and his guide couched the camel so that the man could dismount. I could have sworn I half-recognised him. Then, when he walked up to me, grabbed my hand, shook it and said, 'Mr Hudson?' I knew I recognised him. But how did he know I was here? No one knew where I was and what could be more infuriating, when you are quite happily losing yourself in the desert, than to be found by the assistant bank manager from your local branch? He held out a letter for me.

'I have been sent out here to inform you that you are currently precisely £23.15 overdrawn and we would like a remittance from you as soon as possible.'

Ahmed came up to me, gave me Jemel's rope, pointed ahead to the direction in which I should keep walking, and trotted off to the west. There was no assistant bank manager and no letter, just Jemel, myself and Ahmed, who was rapidly decreasing in size as he ran away from me. My daydreaming really got the better of me that time.

I could not understand what Ahmed was up to. I followed the direction he had pointed in and soon came to a small sand sea but before I disappeared into it I turned round to have a last look at where Ahmed had gone. Now I saw the reason for his sudden departure. Far away, almost out of view, was a small train of camels, heading in the opposite direction. Ahmed was nearly upon them. Then I was into the dunes. I tried keeping a straight line but it was difficult; the dunes always tried to steer me on a course of their choosing. I was not worried about getting lost, though: Ahmed would be able to find me. Desert people are experts at reading tracks. They can tell from the tracks of a party of camels not only how many there are, but in what direction they are going, how long ago they passed, the age and sex of each camel, their breed and size and their weight, so determining whether or not they are laden or mounted. If they also inspect their droppings they can tell how long ago they had a drink; when, and perhaps where, they were last eating pastureland; and what state of health they are in. From all this accumulated information they can make calculated guesses as to where the camels come from, who they belong to, how many people are travelling with them, what sort of business they are about and where they are going. Ahmed was certainly not going to have any difficulty following my walking-shoe tracks. The floor of the desert was an open book, it held no secrets for the learned reader.

Coming out of the sand sea some time later, I saw three large herds of sheep approaching across a short, flat plain. They shimmered and wavered in the heat haze and when I drew close to them the sound of their many thousands of feet rustled like a forest of leaves in the wind. Behind each herd was a young man who ran back and forth, trying to keep the sheep moving steadily in the right direction. I greeted one of them and asked him where he was bound; this being about the limit of my Hassaniyya, I could say little more. I learned they were on their way to Zouerat in the north from Tidjikja in Tagant, a good five-hundred kilometre journey. Ahmed caught up with me here.

A short distance behind the herds of sheep we found a ram lying on the ground, panting. One of the herdsmen came back to try and budge him but gave up and told us we could take him if we wished to. At first Ahmed tried to lead him on a rope but the poor thing was quite finished, close to death. Perhaps he had not managed to get a drink at the last well. Very skilfully, Ahmed managed to strap him on top of Jemel where he lay with glazed eyes and lolling tongue, but he kept slipping and every few minutes Ahmed had to readjust the load. In the end he simply let the sheep fall to the ground and marched on, leaving it to die. It seemed a terrible waste to me, especially in a place where meat was so valuable and food was never

122

unnecessarily wasted. But Ahmed had made up his mind and did not give the sheep a second glance. I mulled over his reasons for abandoning it for a long time.

One of the things that kept my mind occupied during the long marches was thirst. It would come upon me each day after only an hour or two. I did not get into the habit of quenching it because I did not know how far the amount of water we had with us was supposed to stretch. Had I done so I would soon have finished what we had and, anyway, I doubt if it would have made much difference to the sort of thirst I had. Instead I drank once in the morning, once at lunchtime and once in the evening. This was considerably more than Ahmed who drank only in the evening and then only the water he used for washing our cooking implements. But my thirst was a terrible thing. It tortured me. I could not keep my mind off it. If I put every atom of my will into ignoring it, for a short while I would be all right; but as soon as my mind started drifting again, it would be back, infusing my every pore, creating a blind, numbing furnace in my head. It became a desperate battle over which I had no control.

Then, one afternoon, just as I was thinking that I could not bear another minute, another second of it, we came to a well. My relief was indescribable – our *guerbas* were virtually empty – but now I had to face the greatest test of my endurance. The water in the well was quite deep down. Ahmed climbed down to it and started to fill the *guerbas*. It took a long time and there was very little of it. Every second was an agony, like holding a finger in the flame of a candle. I desperately wanted to ask him to send up a little water right now but I knew that I would not do that. I could not crack up and crumble – there were still many more days of the trip to go and, anyway, Ahmed was working as fast as he could and he was not drinking. So I waited. I waited while he hauled up the two *guerbas* on the end of his turban. I waited while he watered Jemel: in the desert the watering of animals always comes first. And then I drank. But, my God, the water was undrinkable, fit only for livestock. I drank a little because I had to, but it made my stomach turn. And our two *guerbas* were now filled with this terrible water. It was all we had. Now, seemingly, I had no way to quench my thirst at all. Not tonight, not tomorrow maybe, not until we came to another well. It was a shattering blow. For the rest of that day I fought a grim and ghastly battle and in the end I began to win. I discovered that the kind of thirst I had was primarily psychological: even if I did drink, it made little difference to the thirst. Ahmed was not drinking and he was okay. I discovered that I had to force it away from my mind, push it down into my body where it produced just a dull roar so that once again my mind became clear and I could think of things other than ice-cold cokes and lakes of chilly water. I had crossed the burning coals and it was not so bad. At least, not all the time.

We came to Aen Savra on our fifth day. It was a poor place, a scattering of stone crofts exposed on a hillside overlooking a ravine with a few thin and lonesome-looking palm trees and a well. Much to my disappointment we did not stop there. We just spoke to the only people we saw, two old ladies sitting outside a house; later I found out that Ahmed was asking where the menfolk were. We passed through the village and walked up some pebbly rivulets in a sand sea beyond it on to another of those indefinite plains of black rock and rubble. After a while, I saw ahead of us the slight depression of a *oued* running east to west and in it was some pale green grass, a thin, temporary coating lying on the hard earth like a mist. It seemed that the slightest breeze would blow it away.

In the depression we found a young man with some goats. Ahmed asked him some questions but the boy was dumb from shyness and only hung his head, grunting. Later on we came to another, larger depression with the same semblance of vegetation growing in it but this time there was small tent next to it. One area was planted with melons, the fruits of a short and meagre rainfall that in a good year gave crops such as this just enough time to mature in the shallow *oueds* where water lay the longest. Far up the *oued* we saw some people. In the late afternoon heat haze they looked like shapes in a surrealistic painting, brightly coloured forms with no heads or legs, wavering and moving, mingling with each other like dancing butterflies over a lake. We walked towards them and when we met, Ahmed greeted them like brothers. They were the menfolk from Aen Savra. Ahmed went off with some of the older men, and a black man with rotten teeth and wild bushy hair took me to see the people harvesting the melons. He could speak a smattering of French.

The harvesters were cracking the melons on rocks and scooping out their insides with a spoon. To my horror, I saw that they were throwing the cool, juicy pulp on to the ground where it became covered in sand and quickly dried out. Still, while they worked they ate and I too was given half a melon with which to quench another of my delirious thirsts. There was a merry, harvest atmosphere. The sun had sunk to the point where it no longer held any strength, and the reaches of black desert were cooling down, no longer such inhospitable places. The men were young and full of jokes and the women round and voluptuous with fine, gypsy faces, buck teeth and prominent black eyebrows. Metal bangles jingled on their arms and red, green and yellow beads were tied round their foreheads. They emitted a strong, musky scent of henna and perfume and their eyes glinted as they laughed.

'Take one of these as a wife,' the man who spoke some French said to me. 'Take two. I have two wives already and I shall take this one here as a third,' indicating one of the women.

'We Mauritanians like to have many wives. They make the best wives, Mauritanian women, and they are v-e-r-r-y beautiful, don't you think? Here, take this one, she likes you, I can tell.' The girl in question gave me a look full of possibilities and they all laughed.

My friend slapped me on the back. 'Ah, yes. She likes you very much,' he said.

That night Ahmed and I sat until quite late with the men from Aen Savra. A dish of couscous was produced, which was a great relief to me as I was feeling really quite unable to eat Ahmed's food with much ease. The men were curious and playful, joking with Ahmed for abandoning the sheep we had left behind. When I asked the French-speaking man to ask Ahmed why he had done so, he gave the simple, noncommittal answer: 'It was the will of God.'

The next day was more than ordinarily testing and the first and only time that Ahmed and I had a misunderstanding. We walked fast and hard in the morning until I noticed that Ahmed seemed to be looking for something. We kept changing course and once or twice went back in the direction we had come from. I began to wonder whether we could be lost. After a while, Ahmed gave me Jemel's rope, and pointing me to walk back along our tracks, ran off in a different direction and was soon lost in the broken landscape. As usual I was tired and thirsty and I started to think of all sorts of terrible possibilities. Had I misjudged Ahmed's character? Where had he gone? The *guerbas* were empty. Was he incompetent, or worse? People in Nouakchott had told me that I should not take a guide into the desert: not all men could be trusted; there were still bandits about. An hour later I was quite convinced that I had indeed been abandoned. Then I saw Ahmed waving to me a long way off. When I got to him I saw that he was by a well. We filled our *guerbas* and set off again.

That afternoon we crossed one of those deserts that was all that deserts are supposed to be: a vast sea of deep, gently undulating white sand in which there is a total nothingness but yourself and your tracks sandwiched between the two burning sheets of sand and sky. Far to the east the plain fell to a sand sea that looked like the tops of a cloud bank seen from an aeroplane. The afternoon was hot and hard. It seemed the sun would never sink. I became more and more weary, trudging through the deep sand hour after long hour. By the time the sun did move into the last quarter of the sky and our shadows pulled away from us, I was raging with thirst and tired enough to drop there and then. When the sun at last set we came to some sand dunes; we entered them and kept walking. It was nearly night and we should be stopping, I thought to myself. Ahmed just kept on and on and I stumbled after him. I cursed him for being so obstinate. I cursed the desert, and myself for being there. I knew why he would not stop – there was no wood to make a fire to cook supper. But I had a petrol burner in my bag. I tried to tell him this but he did not understand. He just kept on walking. I tried again but he irritably indicated that we had not far to go, as if I was telling him to stop. I tried once more, knowing I had to stop as soon as possible, but Ahmed looked confused and annoyed. Then, suddenly, we stopped. Now I was confused as there was no wood here either. Ahmed went off to search and did not return for half an hour. I felt bad because he had had to continue walking and then carry the wood back to where I was, and he looked very tired and not very happy because he thought I had not trusted his judgement of when to stop. But when I showed him my petrol burner, understanding lit up his face and he smiled. A small incident, really, but one that had magnified in importance to the point where I knew I could act irrationally. In the desert one had to acquire the self-discipline that distinguished those who came from the desert. Perhaps one had to have the discipline of Islam. It was born in the desert, it was shaped round the demands of desert life, and the desert is where Islam can be seen in its best and most useful light.

That night I lay for a while, too tired to sleep. There was a half moon and the sand dunes around me were still and silent in its cool light. But as I lay there I realised that in fact they were not silent. The night was silent – utterly and completely silent – but coming from the dunes I could just sense a barely perceptible hissing. Billions of particles of sand were sliding and settling: the secret talk of the desert.

From that day on it was downhill to Rachid. We crossed another sandy plain. We met a few more travellers, crossing like ourselves from one place of settlement to another like ships on a sea. I marvelled at the different colours of sand: pale green, orange, grey, all the shades of yellow and white and even some patches of steely blue.

The last morning was the coldest of the whole trip. We crouched over our fire for a long time before our limbs felt warm enough to set off. That morning we had finished the last of our food and water so we walked the rest of the day without stopping until late afternoon. Cresting one horizon, we came to a plain of scrubby bushes, a sign that we were indeed progressing south, then for a while we wandered in many different directions until Ahmed found the head of a gully. At length this fell to a canyon which in turn led to another, wider canyon with a river of sand meandering at its bottom. Down here at last the desert was shut away. The wind stopped howling, there were knots of palm trees and soon we came to two abandoned stone houses. Later we met a man with an axe. Ahmed talked to him and he led us to his house. He was a blacksmith and we passed the remainder of the afternoon with him and his family. They fed us couscous, a new type of couscous for me, and the blacksmith's daughter and mother showed me some cushion covers on which they were drawing thin, intricate designs.

When evening set in we had a last, pleasant walk up the canyon, passing at the feet of small stone villages sitting neatly on the hillsides. At sunset we came to a place where two tall, cracked headlands of rock stuck out into the canyon, nearly cutting it in two. On a hillside on the far side of one of them was the small town of Rachid, commanding the pass and the canyon that lay below it. This was where I parted from Ahmed and Jemel: they went on up the canyon to Tidjikja and I remained in Rachid. I was in Tagant now, a different strain of desert, a new people, and the end of my walk.

Abid or ex-slave girl, watering a camel in a small *palmerie* on the way to Tintane.

My guide, Ahmed of Chinguetti, making tea on the walk to Rachid.

An old man in a *palmerie* near Chinguetti.

Two Bedu boys near Oualata.

A young Mooress of the desert camps in the region of Tagant. Buck teeth are a sign of beauty here.

Sand dunes and the remains of a *palmerie* on the outskirts of Chinguetti.

My guide, Ahmed, leading his camel through sand dunes south of
Chinguetti.

Sand dunes in the Adrar.

The small cement, box-like houses in which many people now live, amongst the dunes on the outskirts of Tamchekket.

Constructed from tightly woven grass on wooden frames, these *tegits* on the outskirts of Chinguetti give shelter to animal herders.

Sal of Tamchekket and a friend.

A black Mooress with a white Mooress in Tamchekket.

Fishing boats and fish market on the beach near Nouakchott.

An Imraguen fisherman bringing in his catch of mullet. The Imraguen fish in cooperation with dolphins who chase the mullet to shallow waters where they can be netted.

11

Rachid, heart of the Kounta

Rachid was an old town, centre for the large and proud Kounta tribe, and although I could have done with a period of much conversation after my eight silent days in the desert, I did not get it in Rachid. It did not matter too much, because in the next town I went to I received all the attention I could have wished. But in Rachid I found myself staying with a silent family. There was a long dark room that by night closed in round the glow of a single oil lamp. In the room there was the family and myself. A large mother with a baby and a young daughter sat in the shadows at one end, the father of the family, his teenage son and myself at the other, and a boy of about five pottered about between the two. There were mats on the floor and some cushions, and in an adjoining room there were sacks of food and two tin trunks containing clothes and the family possessions. In the yard outside were a number of goats, forever trying to come into the room, and one of the family was continually occupied in trying to keep them out. One of the kids was tied up at night so that it could not drink its mother's milk, which was being kept for the family in the morning. It bleated incessantly during the night and kept me awake. Sometimes the bleating of the kid was joined by the crying of the baby. Then the whole family would make as much noise as possible, banging tins and shouting, to swamp the wailing of the baby and so distract it. Sometimes, in the evenings, the family would tear up old cardboard boxes and mix the pieces with water to be fed to the goats. Once in a while one of the goats was slaughtered and its meat made to last for a couple of weeks.

Each evening, as soon as the sun set, the father would make tea. He was not one of those people who made a great show of making tea; it did not worry him if there was not much froth in the glasses. But he was a thorough tea-maker. He washed all the implements many times during the process and when he had finished he put them neatly back on the silver tray, draped a cloth over to keep off the dust and put the tray back in its place in the corner. Then he would turn on his radio and listen to the messages. They came in a fast monologue with hardly a breath between them:

'Ahmed Ould Akbar of Tidjikja sends best regards to Mohammed Ould N'Darr of Kiffa, Iman Sane of Nouakchott says to Ibrahima Ould Ismael of Auoun El Atrous that his father has recovered from his illness, thanks be to God, Fatima Tomy sends . . .' and so on.

After an hour of this he would turn the radio off and, having covered it with its dust cloth, return it to its proper place. The wife would then stir herself from her end of the room, where she had been nursing her baby, go out into the yard where she had her pots and pans and bring back a dish of couscous. The teenage son would bring a bowl and a kettle of water for everyone to wash their hands. What was left on the platter once the menfolk of the family had eaten would be passed to the wife and her young children to finish as their supper. When this was over the young daughter and son would come over to the oil lamp with their schoolbooks. They would put their books right up against the lamp and hunch over them, reciting over and over again the lines of the Koran that they had been set that day. The father would sit and watch them, making corrections to their mistakes now and again. Sometimes the five-year-old boy would come and disturb them by climbing on their backs and trampling over their books. Then the girl and boy would giggle and the father would gently direct the child back to his mother at the other end of the room.

The father had an old gun. Sometimes he took it out from where it lived, wrapped in a blanket, tucked behind the trunks in the adjoining room. He would oil and polish it thoroughly, then carefully replace it. Being a builder, the father had very rough hands. He often tried to soften them with soap, working up a good lather and massaging it into his skin until there was none left. When the children fell asleep, the mother put them in a line and spread a blanket over them. Not long after this the father would turn out the oil lamp and everybody would go to sleep where they sat and in the clothes they wore, wrapped round in blankets pulled over their heads.

The father was building a baking oven in the yard with a small outhouse round it. He wanted to bake bread to sell. Early in the mornings the men who were helping him would come and sit round a brazier warming their hands, then they would go to work. They made bricks from sunbaked mud and carried them to the father who would position them and slap mud on top of each one. Later in the morning the teenage son and daughter went off to the village school and the mother busied herself feeding and milking the goats, making the couscous for the evening meal, cleaning rice and doing other household chores before she, too, went into the town. By midday everybody would be back in the room. The father would again make tea and the mother would produce a platter of rice. If there were friends who had dropped in, she might produce extra rice and put some of it on a second platter – then the men could eat well and the rest of the family would have their own dish. Afterwards the father would turn on the radio and listen to whatever news there was, and the afternoon would pass idly in dozing and chatting. Once the heat had left the day, everyone would freshen themselves up a bit and go out to socialise before nightfall.

At one time during my stay there was a marriage in the town. You could hear the noise of the marriage party all over town because it was so small, really only a village. The festivities went on for three days, with everybody in the town joining in. On one of these evenings the mother put on her best dress – it was a dress so deeply stained with indigo that it was black and shiny; the indigo came off at a touch – and the father took his gun, and they both went to the marriage celebrations, but separately, the mother with her woman friends and the father with his men friends. The children scampered off with gangs of theirs.

The marriage party was in an open-sided tent with two poles holding it up in the middle. At one end sat all the married women, covered in black from head to toe, only their hands and faces showing, and sometimes not even those. The mother squeezed herself in amongst them. The rest of the tent was packed with everyone else, squatting, kneeling, standing and spilling out of the sides. In the middle sat the Igaouene bard, a proud-looking man with an electric guitar on which he played a long, thin, wavering rhythm with little hiccups and coughs in the sometimes building, sometimes ebbing tunes. There was also a big tom-tom drum, which was beaten by a young woman in a simple, regular rhythm, like a heartbeat. The married women did a double clap for each of the tom-tom beats.

In front of the Igaouene was a catwalk of open space for dancing. Not more than two people danced at a time and always the young, unmarried ones. The young men danced like strutting cocks, with a touch of flamenco, holding their bright blue or white *bobos* out like wings, swirling them around. They stalked up and down the catwalk with jerky motions, now and again holding themselves in awkward poses that they gradually wound out of, like uncoiling snakes. Then they would suddenly fall on their haunches and let themselves go into a wild, well-balanced capering, throwing out their legs, landing on one hand, jutting their heads back and forwards. The crowd would shout and cry encouragement; the married women would set up their high-pitched, ululating battle cry and then the men would suddenly arch their backs, throw their heads back and stare with bulging eyes at the roof of the tent, quivering like taut bowstrings. Soon they would break from this pose and begin the dance again.

When the young women danced they did so much more demurely and elegantly, almost all expressive movement confined to their hands. With their brightly coloured muslin shawls pulled over their heads

132

and faces, they let their hands and fine, long fingers dance above their heads, curving and carving the air in time to the rising and falling beat of the guitar, twirling gently around occasionally, letting themselves go just a little. Then their heads would fall back and their shawls would fall away, revealing young, ecstatic faces. They would slowly spin and lean their bodies from side to side and once again the crowd would rise up in excitement, until the girls pulled their shawls back over their heads and regained their composure. These dances went on for a long time, each one becoming less controlled until, as if that were enough for now, the music stopped and the crowd filtered away. Only the hub of married women remained, clapping to the tom-tom, until later on the crowds were drawn back again.

Night, when it fell on the village, was as dark as a moonless night can be. Nothing could be seen without the aid of a torch or a lamp except the vague, jagged outline of the headland of rock that rose above the village. Under the blanket of darkness the people at the wedding party became more uninhibited, the beat of the tom-tom picked up and the married women clapped fast, piercing the night with their warbling cry. There was a large crowd outside the tent, a press of milling forms with torches and lanterns. Children dashed in and out of the pools of light. The young men had hot, shiny faces, the young women had their shawls thrown back and their best jewellery glinted in the swinging beams of torchlight. They were playful and forthright, displaying a fierce sexuality. There were gun shots as some of the men let off rifles above their heads, flames leaping from the barrels.

Much later on, around midnight, the crowd moved off. In a long, snaking line bearing lamps, it followed the tom-tom and the married women, the people shouting and singing as they wound their way through the small rocky lanes until they came to the home where the bride and her female relations had been preparing themselves all day. They were in a small stone hut like a crypt, all lit up with colourful lights, a sheet draped over the doorway. When this was pulled aside a room deep in cushions, rugs and blankets was revealed,

133

with the forms of people lying sumptuously amongst them.

When the bride emerged she was cordoned round by the married women and they made their way through the village again to a house where the bridal suite had been prepared. They walked very slowly, one small step at a time, with the crowd of villagers following. They did not go straight there but made many rounds of the village, stopping now and again to sing songs. When at last they arrived at the door the crowd stood for a long time, singing and clapping to the tom-tom. It was long after the bride had entered that they moved off to make yet more rounds of the village. I left the party at that stage and returned to the house of the family I was staying with. I found them already asleep. For a long time before I too slept, I could hear the distant cries and shouts of the wedding party coming up the hill from the town.

The people of Rachid were not used to seeing Europeans. Once every few months an expedition of them would pass on their way from the ancient sights of Tagant to those of Adrar, but they would only stop to buy some provisions and then maybe camp in one of the *palmeries* further up the canyon. As a result, whenever I went walking in the village, I was followed by a mob of curious children. One of my more faithful adherents was the small boy from the family I was staying with. Despite his size, he would follow me on long walks up the canyon and became my silent shadow. The only place he could not follow me into was the police compound. I had made friends with the chief of police and his friend and every morning I would go and drink tea with them, and my shadow would wait for me outside.

When I had first met the police chief I had thought he would be a difficult man. He wore mirror sunglasses indoors and out, was silent, and smiled or laughed at the wrong times. In fact, though, he was just a shy man and only smiled so often because he found everything mildly amusing. Everybody respected him and his authority. His friend was a younger man called Said. He had spent a lot of time in Paris and was very suave, always well presented in starched *bobos*. He had a long, sky-blue turban that made him look like a handsome actor. He spoke French perfectly and a little English as well. The two of them had been posted to Rachid for two years and were very bored. They had set themselves up as well as they could in the guardroom.

The police chief gave me a Mauritanian smoking pipe and tobacco pouch and I soon learned the knack of ramming the slim, straight pipe down the pouch then holding the tobacco in with a finger until it was lit. Each stuffing gave only two or three puffs and after each smoke you had to push a steel rod down the pipe to dislodge the ash. The police chief and Said were very adept at it, their hands forever employed, stuffing, puffing, ramming and scraping with a small penknife. The penknife and an ashtray went back and forth, and when I joined the two men we set about this business as if we were craftsmen contructing something of great importance. The tobacco was extremely rough, like tree bark, and all three of us hacked and coughed.

Said was convinced I must be a journalist and would give me long talks about history. 'You *must* learn about our history,' he would exclaim. 'Our history is our present and our future.' It was a bloody history, wrought with the names of fearless, even invincible, leaders, of trouble-making tribes and tribal conflicts. Rachid was the heart of the great Kounta tribe and at one time had had its palm groves cut down to a tree by a neighbouring tribe, who laid it under siege for three years. Everybody had genealogies as long as history cared to remember and these accounted for much, but his explanations were complex and, to me, utterly confusing. There were too many names: the Idaw Aych Emiral family descended from Abu Bakr; Shaykh Ma'el-'Ainin, the famous religious leader of the north; the Rigaibāt and Oulad Ghaylan tribes. In his stories there was bloodshed for territorial reasons, for petty banditry like the thieving of some camels, for the failure to pay blood money. There was bloodshed for the great movements, the Arab invasion and, of course, holy wars. He told me that the women of the camps would smear themselves with excrement to deter the French from raping them when they overran their tents, and that the French habitually insulted the tribes by bathing in camels' milk, near-sacrilege to camel-rearing people.

The police chief did not join in the conversations much, merely adding his favourite sayings now and again:

'The French only conquered Mauritania for the gum arabic,' he would say. And, 'There is nothing in Rachid these days, nothing, absolutely nothing,' smiling calmly as he said it, as if it was almost quaint.

At midday I would leave the police compound. My two friends would try to get me to stay to eat with them and sometimes I would, but then I would have to eat a second lunch with my family, something I would rather avoid as after my desert fare I was having difficulty eating anything, my digestion making me quite feverish at times. The wife was very concerned at my eating habits and went to great trouble to produce food she thought I could eat; noodles, pancakes and, on one occasion, a whole sheep's head. She looked extremely disturbed when sometimes I could eat little more than a few handfuls, as if I must be at death's door.

When I left Rachid, I did so with a rucksack full of presents I had been given by people who barely knew me but who wished the guest to their town to feel welcome. Perhaps the best present was that given by my friend, the cripple. He had no legs and was bright and intelligent and passed his days listening to the BBC Arabian Service in the room he never left. He gave me understanding, a feeling of sympathy that nobody else could because only he knew the fatigue that sometimes comes with always being the odd one out. He would let me sit with him and did not ask too many questions.

12

Tidjikja

I was fortunate enough to get a lift in a very comfortable Mercedes overland vehicle from Rachid to Tidjikja. It belonged to a well-to-do bureaucrat who had come home to Rachid to visit his parents. The route lay along the *oued* of Tidjikja, about forty kilometres, and we sped along at high speed, absorbing the contours of the earth like a hovercraft. The stone villages and long, drawn-out *palmeries* passed quickly. From behind the firmly shut windows of the car and in the air-conditioned atmosphere we were so detached from them that they could have been on a cinema screen. The smooth ride had an adverse effect on some of the other passengers, however, and the three women sitting in the very back grew progressively whiter until a stop was demanded, and they got out to be sick. Fortunately there was a doctor in the car. He had a pet desert rabbit, all thin and bony, on the end of a piece of ribbon and he also had a briefcase in which there were many pills. Once he had administered some of these to sick passengers and healthy ones alike, we were able to continue, only having to stop one more time for one of the women to be sick again.

Tidjikja started as a scattering of square cement boxes on a flat piece of desert beside the *oued*. As we drew closer to the centre of town the cement boxes became more concentrated until there was a maze of tiny alleyways between older-looking, not quite so square boxes. This was the old Ksar and, as these desert towns will, it gave the impression of being deserted.

Across the *oued* from the older Tidjikja was the modern, administrative part of town. It was swept through with sand dunes but was quite extensive, Tidjikja being the capital of Tagant, one of the principal provinces of Mauritania. Set aside from this a little in a grove of prickly trees was the house of the governor. Clutching a letter of introduction, I made my way there to be informed that he was in a meeting by some smart young men who came to see what a rather scruffy and by then quite smelly English traveller with a large pack on his back wanted. I did not want anything in particular, I told them, but just had a letter of introduction to the governor. Later I was led into a very large room. At one end a circle of men, dressed in the lavish and expensive sort of *bobos* and turbans that only big *patrons* wear, were sprawled on the floor. One of them dislodged himself and came over to where I stood by the drape that hung across the door. He was a small, portly man; in fact, the governor. He was important because he was the governor not only of Tidjikja but of the whole of Tagant. Also he came from a powerful *marabout* family who were greatly respected throughout the country. This was borne out by his smile, which indicated not only authority but also humility, like a priest's. He shook my hand, read my letter and took me to a room that he said I could stay in for as long as I wished. He then hurried back to his meeting.

I spent many more days in the governor's house than I had intended and they were extremely pleasant ones. I was forever trying to formulate and organise plans for further travelling. I enquired about the hiring of camels and Landrovers, but they were always too expensive. I enquired about trucks going to some ancient towns in the desert to the east, but every time I was about to leave people would say to me, 'Why leave today? Stay. Stay for a few more days.' And so I did.

Meanwhile the peaceful, almost mosque-like atmosphere of the governor's house and the company of his delightful family lulled me into an idle and contented state. I rarely left his house – only to

promenade and to go to the town now and again to see about arranging
the transport I never took. I had my shoes fixed up once again and
at last I found someone who could cut my hair. I also spent some
time negotiating with the sharp town merchants to change some
money on the black market: I had no local currency left as there were
few banks in the interior of Mauritania, and none that I had so far
come across.

The governor's house was a series of long rooms placed round a
large court. Two of the rooms were reception rooms, each of which
could have held up to two hundred people. They were entirely empty
but for gaudy, wall-to-wall carpeting and thin red mattresses laid
along the sides. There were also a number of guest rooms, the
servants' quarters, kitchens and the family wing, into which strangers
never ventured. The whole place and its grounds were surrounded
by a wall, the far side of which was in many places level with drifts
of sand.

Although it often seemed that the place was deserted, there were
in fact many people in the governor's house. There being no hotels
in desert towns, governors were traditionally obliged to lodge any
travellers or emissaries who had no friends or family in the area. Being
the head of a big family, too, the governor also had many dependants
and family servants who stayed in his house. For example, there was
Ibrahim. He was a young man who was a distant relation of the
governor's and a biology teacher at the local *lycée*. And there was
Salec, the son of the chief of a village which was tributary to the
governor's family. He had something wrong with his joints and his
father had sent him to the governor, hoping that he would be able

to send him to hospital. So far no cure had been found and Salec had been living on the governor's goodwill for six months. The town's police chief was a family friend of the governor's and he was lodging in the house, too, for the duration of his posting to Tidjikja. He was suspicious by nature and of uncertain temperament. Now and again he would send a servant to call me to his rooms, telling me to bring my papers with me. He would study them over a glass of tea and then dismiss me with a dissatisfied air. The governor's children thought him funny and treated him like an uncle.

The governor had four daughters and one young son. The eldest daughter, Aziz, was divorced and had come back to live with her family. She was very beautiful as, in fact, were all the daughters. They were fair-skinned, had finely sculpted noses and lips as soft and well-shaped as petals on a pink rose. Their eyes were dark and dashing, their fingers long and deft and the palms of their hands stained with patterns of henna. They wore lots of colourful muslin that they pulled over their hair like nuns, leaving only a shiny black fringe showing. When they moved they seemed almost to drift, their large, soft bodies swaying gently beneath their robes. I was, needless to say, infatuated with them all but none so much as Nanja, the second oldest. She had the sort of beauty men fight wars over, pure and unblemished. Her laugh was as light as a forest stream, her eyes as moving as jewels, and she teased me with unabashed cruelty.

In the early mornings the three younger daughters pulled their shawls close about them and went to the *lycée*, chaperoned by Ibrahim. When they returned, later in the morning, they would come and see me in the long reception room I was lodging in. I would be chatting with Salec, who had become a good companion, and one or two other people like the young black servant, Abdulahi, a cheery soul who was treated much as a part of the family. Another, older man would often be with us, a black Moor who had come to Tidjikja on some business matter. He was a quiet, thoughtful man. He wore a large brown cape like a highwayman and baggy trousers. He once told me that he did not wear these clothes in Nouakchott: there he habitually wore a suit, but he said that one did not wear Western

140

clothes in Tidjikja – this town was an old town, an Islamic cultural centre and the fief of the powerful Idaw Ali tribe, so one wore traditional clothes in such a place.

The girls would bring into the room with them an atmosphere as of church bells ringing on a Sunday morning.

'*Ça va, ça va, comment-allez vous?*' they would call to us, using just about the only French words they knew. Then they would get down to the serious business of cross-examining the stranger from England who had been so providently provided for them. Salec would do the translating and when he could not make himself understood to me in his poor French, the girls would hit him and say, '*Non, non.* Stupid boy, stupid boy.'

Salec would fend them off and poke them with his finger which made them even more cross.

'Which one of us is the most beautiful?' one of them would ask Salec to translate to me. But I would not fall into their trap and refused to answer, even though they would insist and ask me the same question each day.

'What is the problem?' they would ask. 'Why does he not say? Is it Nanja, or who is it? It must be Nanja, she wants to marry him.'

Even Ibrahim would insist that I answer this question and would become quite annoyed when I refused to. But then he also was infatuated with Nanja. He did not show it, of course, because he was an older, more serious person and she was really only a girl. All the same, it seemed he could not devote enough of his time to her. Whenever the opportunity arose he would be in close conversation with her at the far end of a room, supposedly giving her help with her homework, but from the shrieks of laughter that came from Nanja it did not seem that they were being very serious about it.

Of course Nanja knew that she was the most beautiful and all but said so. The large Senegalese girl who spent a lot of time with the daughters was much more blunt.

'Oh, Nanja, you know you are the most beautiful. You only want to hear other people say so. You're terrible.'

At which Nanja would slap her arm.

'Oh, you're no fun, Fatima. You're just big, fat and ugly.'

And Abdulahi, the young servant, would jump up from the floor where he had been making tea, slap his thigh and laugh, saying, 'Oh, Nanja. You're too much sometimes, just too much.'

Nanja would then say, 'And you can shut up too and go and get us some dates.'

Abdulahi would laugh again and say, 'Either I make the tea or I get some dates. I can't do both.'

So Salec would go and see if he could find some dates.

Sometimes Aziz, the eldest daughter, would come and join us in the reception room. She would settle herself down and Abdulahi would get all the implements for her to make tea. She was a very slow tea-maker; it could easily take up to an hour and a half to get through the three glasses. She would tell her sisters to stop bothering their guests so much and then say to me, as if to reassure, '*Il n'y a pas de complication ici, pas de complication, c'est une bonne maison ici,*' in her good French.

Then she would scold her sisters for not looking after their guests well enough and tell them to go and get us some milk and dates. The dates, when they arrived, were very good and dipped in rancid butter.

Aziz would say to me, 'These are the best dates to be had at this time of year. You know, most people cannot eat these dates. It's only the houses of noblemen who can afford such luxuries.'

And with such idle banter the afternoons would pass. The girls would have to go off later to the women's quarters to be with their mother, but in the evening they would return. Generally in the evening I would go and sit on the verandah at the back of the house. It looked through the grove of prickly trees, over the wall and across the wide stretch of the *oued* to the line of Tidjikja old town.

When the sun set, a long line of camels would come in from the desert where they had spent the day browsing, and drift up the *oued* as if on a conveyor belt. I would sit there smoking my Mauritanian pipe and Nanja would come and sit beside me. She would watch me smoke and say things to me that I did not understand, but '*Hejala*' was a word I knew and one she often used. It meant 'to marry'. She

142

would ask if she could fill my pipe for me. When I let her, the others, who would be sitting further up the verandah, would laugh.

'See, she is his wife already,' they would say. 'She fills his pipe for him.'

And Nanja would give me one of her twinkling looks, half-mock, half-tease, wholly disturbing.

When night fell everyone would disappear for a while, leaving me in the long room with a candle. Later a servant would be sent to ask me to come to the reception room next to the family wing. Leaving my flip-flops by the many others at the door, I would enter to find myself amongst a cosy family gathering. Aziz would be doing some stitchwork, maybe on a small cushion. Ibrahim and Nanja would be at the far end of the room talking quietly and the two younger daughters would be studying their schoolbooks. The mother of the family and the big Senegalese girl would be sitting cross-legged on the floor studying some cowries in front of them. Now and then one of them would sweep them up with a hand and scatter them again. They would mutter over their formation and what they predicted for the future; a favourite game of women in Mauritania.

The mother was a large, powerful woman with small black eyes, not the sort one would want to cross; the sort of wife whom a husband, be he a governor or not, takes much notice of. She was not, physically, a very active woman because of her enormous size but the doctor had advised her to take some exercise each day, and so every morning she would do two rounds of the verandah that circled the house. As I brushed my teeth from the tap on the verandah I would meet and greet her. She would only mutter a greeting back as she would be out of breath, moving slowly like an old sea lion on swollen, painful feet.

The governor's son, Mohammed, would also be in the room. He was a good-looking boy, about ten years old. He had already inherited some of his father's natural authority and correctness, and listened carefully to anything that was said to him. All the servants adored him and he was kept smart and clean by his many sisters and mother in a mini Western suit, making him the only person in Tidjikja, other than myself, to wear Western clothes. We would play a board game of his together. He would play with great seriousness and more often than not beat me. The other people in the room were Abdulahi and other young servants. They would be lying in the middle of the floor, comfortable and languid like cats, joining in anything the others were doing or saying, laughing a lot and getting up to get things for them before they had to be asked.

Later, when the mother and Aziz disappeared into the women's quarters, everyone would gather round to talk together. Sometimes the girls would give me lessons in Hassaniyya. I already had a list of words that I had learnt, some of them given to me by my friend Isslemou, the radio mender in Chinguetti. Or perhaps I should say my mischievous friend, for a few of the words he had given me did not mean quite what he had said. One evening I said one of these words to the girls. They shrieked with laughter and, leaping up to shut all the doors and windows, asked me to repeat it. Again they all fell about laughing and explained to me, graphically, with the aid of a tea glass and a finger, that instead of meaning 'I am content', as I thought, it in fact meant 'to make love'.

The governor would not be there earlier on in the evenings, but would be out about his innumerable duties. He had to deal with all the problems and petitions brought to him by the people of Tagant, each one of whom was entitled to a private audience if they so wished. When he did come home a servant would come and warn us of his imminent arrival. Then the girls would hastily pick up their things and disappear into the women's quarters where, in theory, they were supposed to remain when there were strangers in the house. But the governor was not a strict man and there was little his daughters could not get away with in practice. When he arrived he would find just myself, Ibrahim, Salec and the servants in the room.

I had a very simple relationship with the governor. He was shy of me, as I was a foreigner, and did not know what to say to me, so he said the same things each time we met. I had told him once about my walk in the desert and my eating of kisera there, the millet cake baked beneath the fire. This was apparently a peasant's food and he found the thought of my eating it immensely funny.

'Did you eat kisera in the desert?' he would ask me each time he saw me. Then he would continue, 'Yes, yes, kisera. Ah, kisera, the cake of sand,' and giggle merrily. The other thing he said to me whenever there was an awkward silence was, 'Are you content? Are you content? Good, good.'

When the governor arrived home a plastic sheet would be laid on the floor and a platter of couscous and meat put on top of it. Then all present would eat. Sometimes the governor would come back with groups of professional men; they would greet me politely but look a little surprised to find a European in the governor's house. On one occasion there was a youngish man with a beautifully oiled black beard. He took me to a corner of the room and lectured me for half an hour on Islam. He clutched me by the arm and shouted into my face. 'It is true, it is true,' he kept saying. He seemed quite disappointed in me in the end because I could not be persuaded to profess myself a believer in Islam. Before I went to sleep at night I would talk for a long time with Ibrahim by the light of a candle in the reception room where I slept. Sometimes a servant would appear with a large bowl of milk and tell me it was a present sent from Nanja or Aziz.

Noblemen's houses may be comfortable and privileged places but their everyday domestic functions are not necessarily any better organised than in poorer men's houses; in fact they are probably worse. The nobleman is generally a busy man and his wife delegates responsibility, being involved herself in more important court matters. The running of the house is therefore left pretty much to the servants, and so guests are left at the mercy of their caprice. I say 'servants' because I would not describe them, as Nanja did, as slaves; 'my slaves', she would say. But then Nanja would put people into her own special categories. Hence, when I sometimes questioned her about the culture of Mauritania in an effort to stem her cross-examination of myself, I would get replies to enquiries about, for example, the Nemadi hunter-gatherers, like, 'Oh, the Nemadi, they're just some people who live with packs of dogs and eat antelope, they're like . . . like animals, really.' And about the black African tribes in the south of the country, 'No, no. They're bad people,' she would say, 'they want to make war with us, they want to make a *coup d'état*, they're not good. The lands of the white people are good, but those of the blacks are bad. The people are all sort of, you know, dirty,' she would say, rubbing her hands on her face. 'No, I don't like them at all.'

But 'slave' was a bad word, not only abolished in the country now but also because the title of 'family retainers' would perhaps be more applicable. Still, there was one servant (I shall continue to say) who made life for the English guest quite difficult sometimes. He was the chief servant and a man of much power. He was referred to as 'the chief'. He was short and stocky and had an abrupt, surly manner. He was a determined man. The girls did not like him much as he was always arguing with them. Everybody had to put up with him, though, as he and his family had been the property of the governor's family for a long time and, new laws or not, the traditional law was quite clear; a family cannot misuse or dismiss a family retainer without very good reason.

Each morning, having woken everybody up, including me, the chief would go round with glasses of tea and sticks of bread for breakfast. Generally, when he gave me my stick of bread, he would cheekily break it in two and take half of it for himself. On my first morning he had told me that he would act as my guide in Tidjikja. I managed to persuade him that I thought a guide unnecessary. But there would be new demands each day. He would hear of my plans to find transport and tell me that he could easily arrange them for me for a fee. He would buy cigarettes and try selling them to me for twice the price at the boutiques. Failing in this, he would ask me straight out for tips, which sometimes I would give him to keep him placated. Then one morning he announced that actually it was not local currency he wanted, but French francs. At this point I enlightened him to the certainty that he would receive no more presents from me at all. Next morning there was no bread. My three glasses of tea soon became only two or one. Sometimes he failed to inform me that

146

lunch was being served so I went hungry until supper. Once, when I tried to buy some food in a boutique, who should appear at my side but the chief. When I returned to the governor's house later Aziz remarked that perhaps I did not like the food in the house. It was very insulting to the hospitality of a house to go and buy extra food.

There were many other ways that the chief engineered to make life difficult for me. As it was, the washing, toiletry and lighting facilities in the house were not that simple. To go to the toilet and wash one needed a bucket to get water from the tap on the verandah. The only bucket the chief made available to me had a hole in the side about one inch from the bottom. This made the process difficult

and somewhat humiliating, having to dash back and forth from the bathroom to the tap, being able to wash only one limb at a time. And the nights being candlelit, I depended on him to keep me stocked with candles; hence I spent many nights fumbling around in pitch darkness. But all these little things were as nothing when I was with the charming family and their friends. Then my silent battle of wills with the chief would seem as irrelevant and petty as a mosquito bite and the girls would feed me up on milk and dates as best they could.

Sometimes in the afternoons I would go for a short walk with Salec, who hung around the house all day, bored. We would have to walk very slowly because of his bad joints. We would go to see the *palmeries* and vegetable gardens and on one occasion he took me to see the grave of a French army officer. He was called Xavier Coppolani and his grave was in the middle of the administrative part of town, somewhat blown over with sand.

Coppolani was a name that often cropped up in conversations in Mauritania, for he had been the man behind the defeat of the Moors by the French, and so the instigator of the colonial era. He had been well versed in the laws of Islam and a great military strategist. He had also, by all accounts, been a man of considerable charm. Under his direction the 'pacification of the Western Sahara' took the form of offering the many tribes the choice between 'co-operation with financial reward or resistance with military consequences'. Skilfully, exploiting traditional rivalries and frictions between the many tribes, he caused much hatred and confusion and before long had nearly as many allies as enemies. The war against the southern emirates was long and cruel and so successful that it was not long before Coppolani became regarded as invincible. Then he took Tidjikja, the bastion of the southern tribes, and finally had a foothold from which to conquer the remaining stronghold of the Adrar. On the night of 12 May 1905, though, a group of men led by a powerful religious leader crept up on Coppolani as he lay asleep in his tent in the French camp in Tidjikja. They entered the tent and, drawing their knives, stabbed him to death. So ended Coppolani and for a while new hope was born in the tribes of Adrar. Coppolani had had good officers under him, though, and implementing his clever strategies they soon conquered the Adrar, and Mauritania fell under French rule. Coppolani's grave looked lonesome here in the midst of his enemies, but although it was somewhat neglected, it had not been destroyed or forgotten.

There was another, much more important grave near Tidjikja. This

148

was of Abu Bakr. He had been chief of one of the old Berber tribes of the western Sahara and had taken over the leadership of the Almoravid army after the death of its founder, Abdullah Iby Yacin. It was Abu Bakr and his lieutenant, Yusuf ibu Tashfin, who ordered the proud men and their camel mounts of the Sanhaja Federation of the southern tribes against the Maghreb on their long path of conquest that eventually extended the rule of these western Saharans from the Senegal to the Ebro in Spain. He cannot have been happy to be buried so close to the man who conquered those of his people who had conquered so much themselves.

One day I went with Salec to the hospital to see a doctor I had met in the governor's house. When we got to the main gates we found they were locked and the guard was nowhere to be seen. Not wishing to be defeated in our purpose, I suggested that we climb over. Salec found this notion particularly strange and funny.

'But you can't do that,' he said, laughing. 'If a guard saw you he might shoot you.'

So we waited until the guard turned up and let us in. The doctor had spent some years in London and could speak good English. We talked of London and his present hospital. It had been built by the Kuwaitis and was run directly by them: there were no intermediary men in Nouakchott, the doctor explained. The Kuwaitis had trained and provided the staff, some of whom were Egyptian rather than Mauritanian, and somebody actually came all the way over from Kuwait to pay the salaries and bring the money with which the hospital survived.

'This is a much better way to give aid,' the doctor said to me. 'In this way nothing can be stolen because nothing goes anywhere near the ministers and those who surround them in Nouakchott. Look what we have. A good hospital where everything is modern and everything works.'

One day I was in town for some reason when I bumped into Nanja going into a house. She invited me in to meet some friends of hers. In the house were a few very smart young men in dazzling white *bobos*, preening themselves in front of hand-mirrors and dabbing

149

themselves with perfume. We had some tea. The young men lounged in the most casual manner on expensive cushions and rugs, lobbing their glasses back to the black woman in a corner who was making tea, as if they were throwing pennies to a beggar, then dismissing her. She scuttled out like a frightened mouse. At first the young men were a little unsure of a foreigner in their perfumed midst but Nanja, with her light-spirited manner, soon had us all laughing together. Later on, having once again checked their perfect appearance like pilots checking their instruments before take-off, they stepped out to go on a promenade, taking me with them. We went to the *lycée*. It was between classes and hundreds of young men and women were milling about outside the classrooms. They looked as though they could have been students in the centre of Paris but my appearance amongst them caused a riot. I was mobbed and pushed about so much that the young men I was with decided we had better leave. We wandered round the perimeter of the *lycée* instead, moving slowly with our hands behind our backs from one group of girls to another. The girls were all dressed in the height of modesty and the young men joked with them as they chatted them up.

Towards the end of my stay in Tidjikja I went for a long walk up the *oued* and out into the desert. As I walked I suddenly found myself infused with new vigour. I wrapped my turban round my head and stepped forwards, drawn on by those bare horizons that always seem to promise something new, to challenge like a fierce mistress. I let my mind wander as freely as my feet, wishing to get out under the stars and the sun once again, to temper myself against the closest one can get in this life to where there is no pretence, no subterfuge, no complex, just yourself and your temptress, battling it out by day, and by night falling tired and worn and lovingly together, pressed fast against each other under the eye of the stars. I decided that the following day I would leave Tidjikja.

I am always sad to leave a place I have got to know, but I was never so sad as when I took my departure from Tidjikja. I rode in a rack above the cab of a big truck. The wind was blowing hard and

I wrapped myself in my turban so that the world was only a thin slice seen through its folds. For the first hour or so my mind was with the governor's family and the friends I had made. The ride was hard, though, and soon it was all I could do to concentrate on staying in the bucking rack and trying to protect my bottom from the beating it was taking. We passed a few windblown villages and then, in a valley, we came to a brown town next to a lake below a cliff face of golden sand. There were groves of big trees here and knots of fresh-smelling vegetation that reminded me of more tropical lands. Later we came to the top of a sheer escarpment that dropped down to the patterns of a round town. While the sun set, and for a long time afterwards, we sped south across a plain of packed sand like a beach, following the line of some hills to the west. The wind was strong and I hung on with my ebbing strength. Then, suddenly, with a large bump that was nearly my undoing, we hit a tarmac road. This was the main hard road in Mauritania, one of the very few there are. It ran from east to west across the south of the country. This was the thread of the more modern world from which was growing a different Mauritania, a place I wished to go to. For now, though, as these roads will, it drew me along it to its focal point, to its point

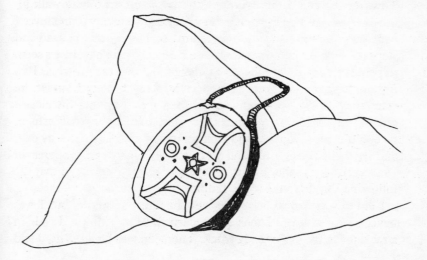

of birth, back to Nouakchott, a brush-up and an excursion up the coast.

I had completed a big circle and in a day's time I found myself facing my friend Sekouba through the pigeonhole window in the reception area of the hotel I knew so well. He was delighted to see me.

'Where have you been?' he asked.

'In the desert,' I replied.

'And how is it there?' he said.

'Very nice,' I said.

And with that he knew all he wished to know about the desert.

PART THREE

JOURNEYS IN MAURITANIA, THE NATION

13

An excursion up the beach: fishermen and soldiers

I sat watching two smiths at work in a market street on the outskirts of Nouakchott. Their workshop was like a coal cellar, a big pile of charcoal in one corner and the floor deep in charcoal dust. Everything in the room was black, including the smiths, who looked like miners just up from the pit; the only difference was that they had bare feet.

They were so absorbed in their work that they did not notice me sitting watching them. One of them was scrunching a pile of soot on the floor in his hands to break up any lumps that had formed in it; the other broke a large, flat cross of aluminium with a hammer. It snapped easily into about ten short pieces which he put in a rusty steel dish like a Chinese wok. He then surrounded the dish with charcoal and with a pair of goatskin bellows he blew the charcoal until it was red-hot, the nose of the bellows buried deep beneath it. Little sparks flew out as he pumped. The other man, meanwhile, had formed a large, smooth, round pat of charcoal dust: taking another flat aluminium cross, he carefully dropped it on top of the pat. Then he put more dust on top of the cross and, with a long wooden stick like a broomstick, he hit the soot all the way along its surface until the pat was once again firm and flat, this time with the aluminium cross sunk compactly inside it. Next he took a teaspoon and removed the dust from the surface of the aluminium, delicately smoothing it down on the edges so that they were exactly level with the surface of the now exposed top of the cross.

He then put four rectangular steel plates neatly over the four ends of the cross and put a square wooden box with a small central hole in its base over its middle section, its edges resting on the ends of the four steel plates so that it covered the cross without disturbing his dust pat. He then filled the box with charcoal dust, holding a round stick in the middle down to the hole in the base and compressing the dust by standing in the box and trampling it down as though he was treading grapes. When it was firm he withdrew the stick, leaving a hole all the way down to the aluminium cross. Carefully he lifted the box off the cross and extracted the steel plates. Still without disturbing the mould, he very gently levered up the cross with a knife and removed it, leaving an indentation of it in the charcoal dust. Now he spent a long time with the knife, perfecting the edges and the bottom of the indentation; then he sprinkled some white powder over everything. Having finished this, he replaced the metal plates over the ends of the indentation and put the square box with its central hole in the dust back over the middle of the indentation, resting again on the ends of the steel plates. He now had a perfect, enclosed mould of the aluminium cross. The other foundryman had by this time melted the pieces of the cross he had broken, renewing the charcoal several times in the process, and was now ready to pour the molten aluminium through the hole in the dust box to form another cross. Unfortunately at that moment I had to leave, so I never discovered why they had broken an aluminium cross only to remake it after a lot of careful work.

The reason I had been sitting watching the men work was that I was waiting for a Landrover to have a puncture mended. I was on my way to visit a fishing village north of Nouakchott and the Landrover had been so overloaded that it had only gone a hundred yards from its starting point when one of its tyres blew out. There were eighteen men on board, one woman, a young girl and, on the roof, a boy and a sheep; it was, I should add, a long-based Landrover. In fact everyone was quite relieved when the puncture occurred: we had already been sitting in the Landrover for an hour before it moved and although everybody in it but me had the prospect of a three-day journey to Nouadhibou through the desert, we were already extremely uncomfortable, overheated and fatigued. Everyone piled out and stretched and some of my companions watched the smiths with me in their forge opposite the spot where we stopped.

The fishermen I was going to visit were called the Imraguen and they lived in the village of Nuamghar. Some people say they are descended from the original inhabitants of the Sahara, the Bafour, who lived there before the Berbers and Arabs came from the north. I wanted to visit them because I had heard that they had a special relationship with dolphins: they used them to help catch their fish. The Landrover was due to drop me at Nuamghar and then continue on its way to Nouadhibou.

The entire one hundred and fifty seven kilometres to Nuamghar were driven along the beach, as there was no road. During the journey we passed several small fishing villages, a military post and two men rolling a tree trunk. The fishing villages were like islands: desert lay behind them and the sea before them. They had a few wooden boats pulled up on the beach and many tables used for drying fish but the houses themselves were made from the flotsam and jetsam of the sea, and corrugated iron. They looked like shanties. The military post was a solitary, frayed tent which disgorged some shabby soldiers who checked our papers.

We had to drive as close to the sea as we could, as that was where the sand was hardest. It took us six hours to get to Nuamghar; six hours of tracing a line of retreating surf; six hours of disturbing colonies of seagulls sitting in our path; and six hours of wind and spray as our outside wheels caught the running ends of the waves. The seagulls would rise up at our approach in a long line that steered out over the sea and then circled round on itself before uncoiling and settling in our wake. Sometimes the birds would be a little late in clearing our path for us and then our windscreen was filled with the shapes of wings and beaks and beady eyes as they rose in confusion.

157

There were three shipwrecks along the coast, each one in an increasing state of decay, the last merely wave-washed ribs sticking out of the sand. In one place a headland of rock stuck out into the sea. Fortunately the tide was quite low, so by judging the waves we could nip around the end of it, but still a small wave broke against our side.

The passengers in the Landrover were filled with horror that I should be stopping in Nuamghar and not going all the way with them to Nouadhibou.

'But where will you stay, what will you eat? There are many military people there,' they said, ominously. And indeed our reception in Nuamghar did make me want to get back on board the Landrover, even if it meant committing myself to the two days of hell the other passengers still had to endure. But I stayed.

Nuamghar was as desolate as any populated place can be. Whereas further back up the coast the desert had been tall, rolling sand dunes that met the sea, here it was just an extension of the beach turned brown with dried mud, and running inland to the horizon without a flutter. On the dried mud was a collection of the same sort of shanties as in the other villages and a few more substantial cement box houses.

The moment we stopped a tall, handsome soldier came over, ordered me out of my place in the front, got in and told the driver to drive on. I just managed to catch hold of the departing end of the vehicle. We went to a small building set a little aside from the rest of the village. Here the tall soldier sat himself down at a desk in an office and ordered the passengers to come in one at a time. Each had his papers looked at, was shouted at and then dismissed. When my turn came I informed the man that I wished to stay in Nuamghar. He seemed a little taken aback but laughed unpleasantly and told me to go outside and wait for him. As I sat outside I felt rather like a schoolboy waiting outside the headmaster's door. The other passengers kept away from me as if I was infectious. They gave me looks that said, 'We told you so, you should have come with us.'

I soon learned that the name of the tall, handsome soldier was Akbar and that he had a sidekick called Omar. There were many soldiers in Nuamghar: even the prefect of the area was a soldier. There were also some marines who had smart uniforms but no boats. All of them were intensely bored and not happy about being posted to a place as desolate as Nuamghar. Akbar had a great sense of humour and thought I might provide some entertainment, so he lodged me in the guardroom with himself and a couple of other men. He informed me that I had come to Nuamghar illegally, as I had no permission to be there. He would keep a close eye on me, he said, until the prefect, who was away at the moment in Nouadhibou, returned and decided what should be done with me. He thought this quite amusing. He also thought it amusing to inform me that as there was no fresh water in Nuamghar and all the water they had came from Nouakchott, making it very expensive, I would not be able to wash during my stay there. What was I going to do about going to the toilet? The customary Mauritanian habit of using the desert was strictly forbidden in Nuamghar, he told me.

'The sea?' I suggested.

'Very difficult,' he laughed, unpleasantly.

Of course he was only amusing himself and I was put up quite comfortably in the guardroom where there was a barrel of water from which I could take as much as I wished. When I explained that I wanted to see the Imraguen, he merely pointed to a scruffy-looking urchin nearby and said, 'There you are, what do you think?' and laughed again.

That first evening Akbar and Omar took me on a promenade, donning their *bobos* in place of their uniforms and wandering about the village with their hands behind their backs as if they were generals inspecting the barracks of their regiments. They took me into one of the fishermen's houses. Inside it had bare earth floors and was low and dark like an Aladdin's cave, with one small room leading to another. The ceilings and makeshift walls were hung and strung together with fishing nets and tackle and oars. Inside one of the rooms was a wrinkled old woman stirring a big pot on a fire. Akbar told her to give us some of the stuff she was stirring and she obligingly doled out a ladleful. Akbar told me that it was the oil of pure fish

159

essence. He and Omar drank some and gave the rest to me. It was very strong and quite disgusting.

'Drink, drink, it will do you good,' Akbar shouted, his habitual manner of speaking.

'Drink up, go on. You're not scared, are you?' chipped in Omar.

I drank what I could.

'Ah, now we must take some exercise,' boomed Akbar.

'Yes, exercise is very good,' repeated Omar.

'This stuff is very strong,' continued Akbar. 'One must get it to circulate through the body or it will make you sick.'

And so saying we left the house and set off away from the village, marching at a good pace out into the desert.

'Run, run,' Akbar said. 'We must let it circulate. It is very good for you. It clears the system. It will get rid of everything in your stomach, even those things that have lain there for years. Of course, for us it is different. We take this stuff regularly, but tonight *you*, you shall cleanse yourself thoroughly,' he shouted cheerily.

'Yes, tonight you shall be very busy,' Omar repeated with glee.

Sure enough that night I had to make many a dash into the desert behind the guardroom where I slept.

On the way back from our walk in the desert we met a girl coming towards us, a pretty, round girl. Akbar barred her way, not letting her pass.

'My beauty,' he said. 'Why are you in such a hurry? Stay and talk to us for a while.'

The girl tried pushing through.

'What's the matter?' Omar said, blocking her. 'Don't try to escape us.'

'What's your name?' Akbar asked. 'Tell us where you live and I'll come and see you tonight, if you're lucky.'

But the girl said nothing and tried to push past.

Akbar stood aside, saying, 'Oh dear, my beauty, what a fierce one you are,' but Omar persisted in blocking her. 'Come, come, what a temper you have,' he mimicked Akbar. But then he let her go and she hurried on to where her mother was waiting.

That night I went visiting with Akbar and Omar, to take tea with some fish merchants who lived in one of the cement houses and then to one of the fishermen's shacks. Inside were two or three very pretty girls. Akbar lay himself out like a master in his harem and proceeded to tease and joke with them. They were unimpressed, but when he grabbed and slapped and tickled them they giggled and made only weak efforts to escape. Omar did not have quite the same effect. When he caught at them in his turn they fought wildly to break free but he held them firmly and thumped them hard on the arm each time they struggled.

'They are very beautiful,' Akbar said, 'and quite willing. Here, you can have this one. Go quickly now or I will have her instead.'

'But are you not a married man?' I said to Akbar, trying to get back at him for embarrassing me.

'Ah, I am married, yes. But I have been divorced seven times. If I want this girl I shall make it eight,' he said. 'This is the way we do things in our country. Tell me, is it really true that a Christian must stay with one wife for his entire life?' he asked accusingly.

'Yes,' I replied.

'Even if he does not like his wife?'

'Yes,' I said.

'What a strange custom,' he said, 'it must be most . . . unhealthy. Divorce is very easy for us,' he continued, with an ugly laugh. 'We are not fools like you Christians.'

Early next morning I went out to see the Imraguen. The village seemed deserted. Each house had an enclosure of fish netting next to it, upon which were hung the splayed bodies of dried fish. Many of the houses had Landrovers parked next to them but there were very few people, so I went to the beach. Further along, on a point of land, I saw a large group sitting on the ground. I approached them slowly because it looked as if they might be praying, but when I got closer I saw that they were just sitting about. All around them were fishing nets looped on to short wooden poles. I walked up to them, greeted the first man and sat down with them. Next to me was a

161

young man. I asked him what the people were doing. Luckily he spoke French and replied that they were waiting for the fish.

My luck must have been in, for no sooner had he said this than a man called out that the fish were approaching. I had been told in Nouakchott that the Imraguen only do this type of fishing at a certain time of year and even then only on some days. For the rest of the year they fish from boats, or not at all. I had been told that all I would probably get from visiting them was diarrhoea. I did get diarrhoea, but I also saw them fishing. The man who had called out was pointing to a piece of what looked to me like flat, undisturbed sea but suddenly all the people on the beach jumped up, threw off their *bobos* and, taking the poles with the fishing nets on them on to their shoulders, walked out into the sea in two long lines. There were boys as young as ten or eleven carrying the nets as well as old men; one old man I noticed was blind and had to be led. Some of the nets were so long that they hung on one pole on someone's shoulder, then looped back to another pole on someone else's, and the two men went out in convoy.

The two lines of men waded out until those in the front were just bobbing heads. Cautiously, the two lines came round until they had encircled a large patch of sea, then quickly the fishermen slipped the nets off their poles and drew them out until the patch was encircled with nets hung from cork floats and weighted at the bottom by pieces of lead. Immediately the sea erupted, hundreds of fish leaping out of the water like missiles, attempting to jump the nets. The water boiled with grey flesh and fins and soon the fishermen could hardly be seen in the turmoil and frenzy. And then suddenly I saw, circling the ring of fishermen and nets, the arching backs of dolphins, skimming and surfing, twisting and turning after the mullet that had managed to escape. It was an orgy of feasting and catching and it lasted about ten minutes, gradually lessening towards the end. The dolphins disappeared as quickly as they had appeared and the fishermen began to thread their nets back on to their poles, dragging them to shallower water where they put them on their shoulders, took up the strain and rose up to run quickly up the beach, muscles

162

bulging and veins throbbing under the weight of fifteen or twenty large grey fish hanging in the nets by their broken necks. Far out to sea I saw the skimming backs of a school of fifteen to twenty dolphins.

Once back on the beach the fishermen set about untangling the fish from the nets and then threading the nets back on their poles. They were in high spirits, shouting and laughing about the catch and squabbling over their share. They were tall, strong people with vivid, well-carved faces, not unlike the Moors. They had wild bushes of hair, often gone grey even though they might still be young. Many of them bore thick seamen's beards. They were grizzled and tough and took no notice of the foreigner in their midst.

Not long after the catch people started arriving from the village, many of them soldiers, to buy some fish for supper. There were merchants, too, who were going to take the fish to Nouakchott. I spoke to one old man who had not gone into the sea. He had a smattering of French and he told me that the fishermen announce their presence to the dolphins by hitting the water with sticks. The dolphins round up the mullet from deeper seas and drive them to the beach, where the fishermen can trap them in the shallows, and the dolphins then eat the fish that escape the nets.

'But why', I asked, 'do they not just eat the fish when they find them? Why do they drive the fish to the shallows?'

His answer was probably the best anybody could give.

'Ah, who can guess the workings of Allah? They come, that is all. *Alhamdu' allah' Bismillah!*'

The young man to whom I had first talked came up and told me that the fishermen could get fifty or sixty *ougiya* in Nouakchott for each fish. He was not an Imraguen himself, he told me, but the Imraguen were 'very rich', he said.

'Yes, they have many fish,' I answered.

'No, no,' he said. 'This is not a good catch. The fishing is not good this year.'

As he was speaking some of the younger Imraguen fishermen noticed us.

'Where are your fish?' they shouted to the young man. 'You have no fish, do you, because you are not an Imraguen. Only the Imraguen can do this fishing.' It was said with bravado and agreed to fervently.

'Never would you get me into that sea,' the young man told me. 'Never. It is very dangerous. Only the Imraguen can do it. Sometimes they get badly cut by the mullet's teeth and sometimes bigger, dangerous fish bite off someone's arm. No, far too dangerous. Only the Imraguen can do that.'

I stayed on the beach with the Imraguen for the rest of the afternoon. Most of the time they lay about, sleeping and fooling with each other, then suddenly another shoal of fish would be seen and they would dash out again into the sea. Sometimes there were false alarms and the older men would not even get up. Sometimes the catch was as good as the first one I had seen and sometimes not so good. I occasionally spotted the dolphins far out to sea; when there was a catch they would appear soon after the turmoil began and dart about after the fish. One old man told me that the dolphins do not eat the mullet, but it certainly looked to me as though they did.

When the sun set everybody went back home and I returned to the guardroom. That night two fat mullet were sent up by the villagers. They had been baked in a fire in a not dissimilar fashion to the kisera I had eaten in the desert. The flesh was as pink and tender as that of a salmon and quite delicious. Akbar, a couple of other soldiers and I sat down on the floor to eat them. I had to eat more than I really cared to.

'The Imraguen have sent these here specially for you,' Akbar kept saying to me. 'These people are very good people, eat up, go on, this is for you. The Imraguen always send food to guests in their village.' He talked through the meal, barking the words out to me as if he was angry. 'The Imraguen are very good. Nobody goes without food in this village. If one man has some fish and another none, then what do you think they'll do? Huh, what'll they do? The man will not eat all his fish on his own. No, these people are not like you. No, he will give some of his fish to the man who has none. They are good people.' Despite his brusque way of putting it to me, I could see that he felt some genuine respect for them.

The evenings I passed in the guardroom were tense and fraught. Although the basic hospitality was adequate there was always an underlying strain of scorn, or even dislike and mistrust of me. Akbar purposefully made me feel uncomfortable, although at times he could be more friendly. When at last the oil lamp was turned out that evening it was so dark that I could not see my hand in front of my face; pure ink. The wind rattled the window shutters as the guards snored.

The next day a French military delegation came to visit Nuamghar. All day long preparations went on for their reception. A large tent was erected and filled with new mattresses and cushions that had come from Nouakchott specially for this occasion; the marines and soldiers beetled about the village in their jeeps, organising all that needed to be organised; in the afternoon the villagers were placed in a semicircle at a little distance from the front of the tent. The soldiers and marines were turned out in newly polished shoes and freshly washed uniforms and stood around in the area between the villagers and the tent. Akbar and Omar strutted about, straightening cushions and joking with the women who were cooking food and making many pots of tea in a hut behind the tent. All afternoon the villagers stood there, sometimes clapping and singing to a tom-tom to keep their spirits up. The sun sank and still they stood; the

165

delegation was late. The sun set and still they stood; then the imminent arrival of the delegation was announced. The villagers were told to clap and sing again as three long, luxury overland vehicles swept up at great speed and halted by the tent. The marines and soldiers came to attention in a line. Out of the three vehicles stepped three French families, clutching cameras and Thermoses, buckets and spades and collapsible beach chairs. Putting down their chairs, the fathers drew themselves up and did their military duty, shaking hands with officers and inspecting the soldiers and marines. This completed, the families were shown into the tents, seated on the new mattresses and given bottles of Coke and Fanta to refresh themselves. The villagers broke ranks and were directed to the far end of the tent where they set up a great din, clapping, singing and dancing.

The three Frenchmen were officers of high rank, but they instigated an atmosphere of informality by joking and laughing with the Mauritanians and showing off their children. When the food came, everybody crowded together round the many large platters of rice and boiled lamb. The Frenchmen told their children to eat with their hands.

'But, Daddy, I can't, it's so dirty,' one little girl exclaimed, 'and there's so much sand in the food.'

Everybody laughed heartily, exchanging knowing looks with each other. I was asked to sit next to one of the French families.

'What do you do in Mauritania?' I asked one of the officers. Then, realising that of course I knew what he did, and to help him with his apparent difficulty in answering, I began again. 'What have you been doing?'

'We've been on a camping tour of the desert round here,' he replied shortly. 'We're on our way back to Nouakchott in a couple of days' time.'

The evening seemed to go very well. When the food had been finished the Imraguen villagers stopped their singing and dancing and went home but in the tent there remained an assorted collection of soldiers, officials, village boys and old men, waiting on the every word and action of the French families. Akbar and Omar were nowhere to be seen. The French families managed to remain totally oblivious of this audience and went through the motions of a family picnic. One of the mothers had a baby and the villagers watched in amazement as it had its nappy changed and was placed in a cot that unfolded from something the size of a small tea tray. The child then commenced to wail unheeded in its frilly pink blankets. One of the fathers, a tough, Foreign Legion type, military down to his very corpuscles, made his children take an interest in the audience who showed them their strange clothes and laughed with embarrassment at the children's tactless remarks. One Frenchman then began unloading the overland vehicles and the families set themselves up for the night in the tent, with the greatest of comfort, and the audience was sent away.

That night, while I was sitting in the guardroom having some tea with the soldiers, a man in a smart white *bobo* walked in. Everyone stood to attention. I knew the man. I had been sitting next to him when I ate with the French delegation; he had been very charming and interested in me. He was very well groomed. He was the prefect, returned from Nouadhibou, and he now let his charm slip a little. He asked a few short questions of the soldiers. Then, to me, he said, 'Do you have permission to be in Nuamghar?'

'No,' I replied, explaining that I had been led to believe in Nouakchott that no permission was required.

'We shall see,' he said. 'What are you doing here?'

'I've come to see the Imraguen.'

'Well, then, do you have any papers that prove this?'

'No.'

'Well, how do I know what you tell me is the truth?' he continued, in an unpleasant tone of voice. 'How do I know that you are not a spy?'

There is little one can reply to such a question, so I merely said, 'I am not a spy.'

He told me he would deal with me in the morning – I was to come and see him at the prefecture with *all* my papers. Turning on his well-shod heel, he left the room. I decided that perhaps the next day

167

would be as good a time as any to disentangle myself from Nuamghar. I had seen the Imraguen fishing, was a little tired of the guards and I had made a mistake with the prefect. One does not chat to such a man as I had done the day before without knowing that he is the prefect and showing the right degree of deference. These men are very powerful in their little rural military kingdoms and their egos are as brittle as sticks.

The drive back was faster than on the way out. There were many vehicles filled with French people going at high speed along the beach for weekend picnics by the sea. I felt sorry for the seagulls who had often no sooner settled back after the passing of a car than they had to rise up and circle over the sea for another. Shoals of dolphins followed us as we drove along the coast, as if we were a boat.

The driver of my Landrover had a load of dried fish in the back. When we approached the tented military post near Nouakchott he asked me if I had a knife.

'Yes,' I replied.

'Then give it to me and I shall hide it,' he said. 'The soldiers here will take it if they find it. As it is, I shall have to give them some fish or they will keep us for hours checking the vehicle over.'

Three or four dried fish duly paid, we arrived back in Nouakchott. I was dropped off where I had started the trip and as I walked back to my hotel I passed the foundry. The same two men were at work; in the back of the workshop I saw a pile of about fifteen aluminium crosses. I did not stop to watch them working this time, for I was tired and looking forward to seeing my friends in the hotel. As I walked on I pondered the prefect of Nuamghar and whether he would from time to time wonder what had happened to that odd young man who had been present at one of his little military soirées without his permission.

14

The Road

The Road stretched away in either direction. It did not waver in its course but now and again it disappeared into valleys. Each time it rose out of a valley it was smaller, until there came a time when it did not reappear at all. Then there was the horizon.

An old man sat beside the Road contemplating its surface, not unlike some of the packed gravel plains in the desert, only it was of a light grey colour that he could not remember seeing in the desert. Also, of course, it looked much more solid, more substantial, the gravel set into tarmac the way it was, cambered slightly to each side. It was a pleasing shape. He remembered the first time he had seen the Road, not long after it had been built. He had been taking some camels from Tagant to the Gorgol in the south; grazing had been becoming poor in Tagant even then, that's why he had been going to Gorgol – for the grazing. He had literally stumbled on the Road. He had heard about the building of it, of course, by some foreigners, but he remembered that it had still come as quite a surprise to him. There had been a long march in the desert and then suddenly this; this neat grey surface. He could not remember seeing anything so . . . so out of place, really – of course the desert then had not been what it is these days. Then you could not walk for more than an hour without coming across a herd of camels. And after the rains it was

169

green with tall grass. Yes, those had been good days, days when the desert was alive with camels and people. There had been nothing on the Road when he first saw it, except the rotting carcass of a donkey, he suddenly remembered. Other than that it had been just road, just a grey line going from one horizon to another.

He had found it quite strange, the idea of some foreigners putting a long grey line from one horizon to another, but in those days he had not really thought about the places the Road went to beyond the horizons, he had not known that it was so long it stretched from the east to the west of his country. That first time he had just stepped over it and within a few miles it was out of sight and he had not given it much more thought. When he came back two months later, having fattened up his camels in the Gorgol, he had been surprised by a big truck on the Road. He should not have been surprised, because he had been watching it approach from a long way off, but it had grown in size so quickly and suddenly it had been upon him and he had had to rush off the Road, he remembered with some amusement. It had frightened his camel and he had nearly lost hold of its rope. This was nearly fifteen years ago. It had not been until a few years after that, that things had started to go really wrong for him and his family. It had been bad to watch the desert die before his eyes. Instead of being a desert that could feed his animals it became one that could not. And then he had had to watch his animals die. The ways of Allah can be strange sometimes, he said to himself.

It was then that he had started to think of the Road again. A cousin of his had gone to live in Kiffa, which was on the Road – in fact a lot of people from his area had gone to live by the Road. Yes, even by then it had become a important place, almost as important as the desert. Still, he had thought it a strange thing to do, to go and live on a road – after all, what is a road? But then when he heard how rich his cousin was becoming he thought perhaps it was not such a bad idea after all. It was when his favourite riding camel had died, he remembered, that he had decided to go and see his cousin.

He had thought it was the right thing to do, even though there was some foreigners' food being given to the people in his area. He had not much liked the idea of living off foreigners' food – still, he had not felt quite right about going to live on the Road. Everything happened from north to south, that was how things had always been done. That was how the wells were placed, that was the way we took our animals, the direction of business. And then the foreigners changed all that by putting their Road east to west. There was something so . . . so untraditional about it. But his sons had told him not to be so old-fashioned and of course they had been right. Roads such as these did not need wells and anyway the wells were drying up. He had not properly understood the Road then: after the drought, things had changed – most things came from Nouakchott, not from the north or south. And so the Road had been built and at least they had put it in a good place, not too far south in the Sahel, amongst the black Africans. No, it was definitely a Moors' road. So perhaps it was for the best. Not that he had travelled on the Road much – certainly he had never been to Nema at the far end of it. Sometimes he could not imagine the Road going all the way to Nema, it was unbelievable. He had been to Nouakchott once, though, when one of his sons took him there.

Both his sons had become merchants like his cousin. His cousin was dead now, but it was he who had helped him and his family and set them up in a new village beside the Road where there were many people of his own tribe. They had opened a boutique. He had not taken much part in it because even by then he was a little old. But his sons had taken to it like lambs to the teat, he remembered fondly. They had been good merchants. Yes, they had been very good. Before long his eldest was able to go to Nouakchott and bring sacks of the foreigners' food. Each time he came back he had more. It was very cheap. Now they were rich and lived with their families in Kiffa. The village had been too small a market for them, he noted proudly. Of course it was a little sad that he did not see much of them now, but he had his married daughters near him, and their families and his wife, of course. The village was a good place. Two big Hassans from Nouakchott had houses here. They came each weekend and then there would be lots of camels' milk, because the herders brought the Hassans' herds of camels in for them to see. Not that the herds were up to much these days, being a mere token of what they used to be. In the old days big Hassans like the ones who lived in his village would not have one or two hundred camels, they would have one or two thousand or even more. Yes, it was sad. But then life was much easier and there were so many things that came up the Road. Milk was never a problem – the powdered stuff was all right. With all that foreign food there was never a problem in that direction and even silly things like batteries and radios were nice to have. Not that he did not miss the desert. Now and again his family would go off for a few weeks into the desert to get away from it all, but it was not quite the same without the animals. He missed the camps and the smell of a herd of camels rustling about in the night. He even missed the long marches in a way, not that he knew why. Yes, he did miss the desert when he thought about it, but he doubted his sons did. I might go back there if I could, he thought, but my sons would not come. No, they have good lives by the Road now. Yes, indeed, the workings of Allah are sometimes strange. It is almost as if he does not want us to return to the desert. He has provided the Road.

At this point one of the old man's married daughters came out of a house behind the lean-to under which he lay on a raised dais, and gave him a bowl of milk.

'You want tea now, Father?' she asked.

'No. Later,' he replied. 'The sun is not yet down.'

Just then a Peugeot full of passengers passed at high speed. The old man watched it until it disappeared with the Road.

'Things are changing. So much goes down the Road never to come back and so much comes up the Road that is new. Yes, things are definitely changing. The Road is very strong now.'

The taxi park in Nouakchott had not changed since I was last there. The Senegalese boys were still hawking their cheap wares from Dakar and catching potential travellers in spendthrift moods. One of the passengers who would be travelling in the same Peugeot as myself

172

could not have been a more ideal victim for them. He was bright and cheery and young and seemingly determined to spend all his money before he got home to Kiffa.

'They're very expensive, these trips,' he told me.

He had already bought a long purple turban from which the colour leaked when he sweated, so he had two purple lines down his face. He had a new torch and a pair of mirror sunglasses. Later, after we had travelled for five or six hours and had stopped in one of the roadside eating houses, he outdid everybody with his generosity. Try as they might, the other passengers could not contribute a penny towards our food, so all nine of us ate at his expense. He also bought me not one, but two cartons of milk and even this was not enough. When it came to drinking tea after the meal quite a heated argument broke out, as all the passengers refused to be the first to drink, insisting that the others should go first. Often the glass of tea would be left to go cold while they were at loggerheads. But it would always be the young man who drank last.

The journey to Kiffa was six hundred kilometres along the Road. That journey was a blur, a mad thrust deep into the continent of Africa along a road that was like a thorn driven into its side. Periodically we changed taxis in the bigger towns and the taxis, like a bus, often changed passengers. Images come back to me. Faces of taxi drivers, wily, self-sufficient men of the Road to whom people were only fares. They sat behind their wheels, peering with slit eyes at the glare, chewing their teeth-cleaning sticks, tapping their smoking pipes on the steering wheel and ejecting spittle out the windows to be whipped away by the fierce winds. Three young girls were sitting on the back seat with stony faces, seeing nothing but their tears. They were being sent away from home and had waved long at their parents where they left them standing beside the Road. There was the woman with her young, mad son who kept opening the car door as we were on the move. There was the big, dashingly handsome driver who slapped him across the face each time he did it, then shifted his tailored bulk around in his seat as if he had been insulted.

Visually the journey was almost dream-like but physically it was

173

a nightmare. Shortly out of Nouakchott we came across one of the vast swarms of locusts that were plaguing the south of the country at that time. The dunes on either side of the Road were so covered in their yellow forms that the sand could barely be seen. As we drove along they crackled like gravel under our wheels and the front of the car became a carnage of their destruction. There followed a hundred or so kilometres through the vast sand sea that is gradually moving from northeast to southwest across this part of Mauritania. It was formed into one perfect rank after another, like a giant sea swell with the Road laid on it like a ribbon. Its colours spanned the spectrum and in some of the pale green valleys between the ranks there were small villages, in which old men lay under lean-tos, watching us go by. In one or two bigger towns the Road became a market for a while, quite frantic with merchants and their sacks of merchandise. Further on the surface of the Road broke up for about forty kilometres and we had to make detours on deep helter-skelter sand tracks; fortunately we did not meet anyone coming the opposite way. At sunset we rose up a steep escarpment and came to the remains of some long grass plains with clusters of brilliant white Beduin tents dotted over them. After dark we stopped in one particular patch of blackness for two of our passengers to go and fetch something for the night. Next to the Road was a depression and in this there was a village but you only knew this from the sounds of it, for it had extinguished all its lights due to the billions of insects, most of which seemed to be attacking the headlights on our car. The village was just a steady hum of voices and movements with rising up out of it the high, pure voices of children singing verses of the Koran.

The heat and the strain of travelling in it for twelve hours at high speed made the journey a nightmare, interrupted by prolonged periods of baking beside the Road as our driver attended to the engines of other Peugeots that had broken down. I noticed that he did not stop for any broken-down vehicle as one would in the desert. It was much more tribalistic on the Road: a Peugeot stopped for a Peugeot, a truck for a truck, a Landrover for a Landrover and, say, a Kounta

174

man for a Kounta man. The car became so hot I had to keep my feet off the floor; it seemed as though the soles of my shoes could melt on the metal surface. After nightfall the nightmare increased. The big trucks that plummeted towards us quite blacked out anything around them with their strong headlights. Collision and death at high speed seemed inevitable. The driver of our taxi did not slow down at these confrontations, but just pointed his taxi at the tiny space of darkness beside the truck and dived into it. Sometimes in this patch of darkness we came across other, slower and lightless vehicles, or maybe a man with a donkey and a cart, often just loose animals. We managed to avoid death but many of the animals did not. Carcasses of donkeys, cattle and sheep lined the Road. By the time we arrived in Kiffa, life could never again be viewed in quite the same way.

15

Strange experiences in Kiffa

Kiffa was the sort of place everybody was living in these days, the sort of place the desert was draining into. Most of the people there seemed to be merchants. Camels, cattle and sheep were brought to the town from the surrounding deserts. They would be fed to its people or transported down south, even to Mali, to be traded for millet or sugar or plastic sandals, or they would be sent to the meat markets of Nouakchott. Some grain and vegetables from Kiffa's *palmeries* made it to the markets but the main harvest came up the Road from the port of Nouakchott – sacks of foreigners' food, often marked 'A gift to the people of Mauritania from So and So. Not to be sold.' They kept the merchants in business for a long time.

The night I arrived in Kiffa there was only darkness and extreme heat, even though it was nearing midnight. A soldier who had been in the taxi was whisked off with me, both of us easy prey, to one of the taxi-park restaurants by a man who came up to us and said, 'Come, come to my restaurant. Very good food, no mosquitoes.'

Taxi-park restaurants consisted of a few big, black cooking pots and many mattresses on the ground on which weary travellers passed the night before continuing their journey next day. It was quite correct that the restaurant had no mosquitoes but it did have a large gas lamp, the focal point for a swarm of all the many and weird insects that had been born in the recent wave of humidity. Even at some distance from it, we were well within the zone of insect inundation.

The soldier and I sat on our mats, quite miserable, pouring with sweat and too tired to brush off the mass of creatures that crawled over us. After an hour of this we walked into town where we found two good Samaritan ladies who gave us mattresses and blankets on which to sleep in their yard. In the night I kept waking to the roar of trucks passing on the nearby Road. In my half-dreams I thought they were bearing down upon me. In the morning I watched the universal scene of family torture: small, naked children were hauled off like sacks to a room to be washed. Even those not going through this ordeal wailed in sympathy with the terrible wails that came from the room.

The soldier that fate had thrown in my way was a quiet, nervous man, on his way back after leave to his posting to a town called Tamchekket, about a hundred and twenty kilometres north of Kiffa in the desert. I was looking for a place north of Kiffa to go to, I said. If he did not mind, perhaps I could accompany him. That was a very good idea, the man replied, but the problem was transport. It might only be a hundred and twenty kilometres away but the piste was very bad and we might have to wait a few days before a vehicle went there. As it happened we only had to wait a day and a half.

Meanwhile, I found out that there was a group of American Peace Corps volunteers in Kiffa and I decided to go and see them. I wanted to ask about this part of Mauritania and perhaps be able to formulate some sort of plan of action for my travelling. They lived in the centre of Kiffa in a house surrounded by a yard and then by a wall, much the same as everyone else in town. When the door of the yard was opened for me I was somehow quite surprised to see about ten young Americans hanging around the place, quite as though it was a university campus. I was not expecting it in the middle of hot, dusty Kiffa, but they were not surprised to see me. In fact my entrance did not seem to rouse any interest at all, just as it would not if indeed it had been a university campus. I simply drifted around, saying 'Hi' to people, wondering if I would get a response.

178

'I wonder', I asked a likely looking girl squatting on the floor sewing buttons on a shirt, 'if you could tell me something about this part of Mauritania?'

She looked confused so I brought out my map and pointed enthusiastically to places, asking if she had visited them. She was not an easy conversationalist. Drawing information from her was like asking spies to tell you their secrets. She looked drawn and overworked; in fact, as I looked around me, all of them looked tired, terribly tired. The house was a mess, the people scruffy and on edge, like people who have just about had enough. Gradually I drew a small circle of girls about my map and now and again one of them would divulge some information, only to clam up again as if in some way I was a threat. Then a young man walked in. He still had some life left. He told me many facts about the planting of crops, the rainfall and the Moors.

'The young men don't like to get their hands dirty,' he said. 'Very difficult to get people to work with us on our projects. Like to watch us do the work, they do,' he said.

There was a much older lady in the house, the mother of one of the girls, on a visit to her daughter. She offered me a glass of water.

'Don't worry, it's been purified and filtered,' she said. 'We have to do that all the time where I live,' she continued in her broad southern drawl. 'Nepa-al, you know. Not far from the Go-obi desert. I go there often. Such a real place. And those nomads, they're just so-o quaint. I do just adore nomads. This place isn't bad. But the Go-obi, you just must go there when you can. What a culture.' She continued for a while on the theme of culture. After a time I took my leave, feeling a little disconcerted because I knew that I was looking forward to being back with the Mauritanians. The young Americans were brave people, though. It must be hard to do their job, and very hard to remain American in the middle of Kiffa. But then it was not that easy sometimes to be anything in Mauritania but a Moor.

The whole of the centre of Kiffa was a market. Every street was a market and every door opened on to a boutique. The streets were filled with boys and their 'chariots', as the donkeys and carts were called, transporting merchandise or merely doing nothing but squabble with each other and bash their donkeys with lengths of steel drainpipe. There were men hauling girders, brick makers, shoe makers, herdsmen with flocks of sheep, the occasional camel, trucks disgorging sacks into boutiques and a general confusion in the streets where they became a part of the workshops and the boutiques became a part of the streets. Every corner had its knot of Moors talking together, and old women set up stalls under pieces of tent in the middle of everything, selling water and milk and sweets and cigarettes to the busy merchants and their workers. The press of business ebbed and rose like a tide drawn not by the moon but by the sun, which at midday cleared the streets of all but the dusty old women dozing like dolls, slumped where they sat.

In one of these streets was the place from which the Landrover for Tamchekket left. The Landrover was not there when I arrived but this was where it would be and where I had to wait. A boutique owner nearby, seeing me sitting in the street, invited me into his shop for some tea. He was a large man with a flat nose, a comfortable belly and a benign smile.

'Come in, come in,' he boomed at me. 'Come in to drink some tea.'

His name was Mustapha and in the time I knew him he only once let that gracious, slightly amused smile of his slip. We had tea and peanuts and he told me about the price of some of the merchandise in his shop and about a German who was a great friend of his.

'He came to stay with me once,' he said, 'and I gave him the best hospitality and so he came again. I always give the best hospitality. I am a Muslim,' he continued, 'so I give good hospitality. Mark my words, I am not like so many people who give good hospitality and in fact want something back. No, I give it with no strings attached,' he declared, 'free. Ah, the beauty of the faith knows no bounds.' He sighed and broadened his smile for a while, so that he looked like the most contented man on earth.

At midday Mustapha closed his shop and asked if I would be kind enough to accept some of his hospitality and pass the afternoon with

180

him and his family. He lived a half-hour's walk out of town, next to a small *oued* which had a little water left over from the rains. He was in the process of setting himself up very comfortably there. He explained that he had lived in Kiffa since his youth but now he wished to get away from it all, so he was building this place. There were two or three wells, some plots of millet, a 'hangar' – an open-sided house – and two good big tents, all surrounded by newly planted trees. His servants were at that moment in the process of building another hangar for him, using pickaxes on the concrete-hard earth, baking themselves in the harsh sun.

Mustapha was surrounded by family: his parents and children; his brothers, uncles and aunts; and also by the animals he still kept – a few goats, a camel and a pack of dogs. We passed a very pleasant afternoon, eating a special dish of choice bits of meat and then rice. I was given many bowls of milk and passed the hours chatting to a young teacher about the threat of the West to Mauritania, as he put it.

'We must be very careful,' he said to me, 'and keep an eye on our culture or we will become like you – very good, I'm sure,' he laughed, 'but not us.'

Mustapha, meanwhile, played with his servants' children. They grinned nervously at him. They were like putty in his large, powerful hands. Later in the afternoon, when we returned to town, I met my soldier friend at the departure street point. He was in quite a state.

'But I've been looking everywhere for you,' he stammered to me.

When I pointed to Mustapha and told him that I had very kindly been invited to see his house, he became very silent.

'I see,' was all he said.

When night-time came round and the Landrover for Tamchekket was still nowhere to be seen, Mustapha told me that I must come and spend the night with him. After I had accepted his invitation, my soldier friend appeared and told me that he had found nowhere to stay the night as yet, but that when he did I must of course spend the night with him. I explained that Mustapha had invited me and hinted that perhaps he could also come and stay the night there.

'He is a very serious man, that,' the soldier said to me, 'very serious. Very good, I'm sure, but I can't come to stay with him because . . . because . . .' After a lot of prevarication he told me he could not explain the reason in French.

Of course I knew the reason. He was not only a soldier, the means by which the military government kept the regions in check, but he was also a man in an area that was not of his tribe. Such a man in the eyes of someone like Mustapha did not hold much merit.

'You must stay where you wish,' he finished in some confusion and then made off, looking decidedly unhappy. I decided to stay with Mustapha, which was a mistake.

Back at Mustapha's homestead he was full of his 'My hospitality is free' business. We ate some food and then sat around an oil lamp outside the hangar. The night closed in upon us, dark and silent. Mustapha sat beside me, big and strong and intense. He went on for a while about hospitality being a gift one can give away freely but all the time I could tell he was working his way round to something. Then it came.

'Peter,' he said. 'When I first saw you I fell for you, you made my heart lurch. There, I said to myself, is a good man, the right man for me. Truly, you made my heart lurch. This is the man I can ask the one thing I desire. As I have explained, I am not the sort of person who asks things of people; nor ever do I, except now and again, when I come across the right person, and you are right for me.'

He said all this close to my face, clutching my arm and staring deep into my eyes.

'But before I ask you,' he continued, 'you must listen to me, listen to what I have to say. I do not force you to, but I know you will grant me my wish when I have finished, so please listen to me. You will, won't you?'

Naturally I had to agree but I looked around anxiously, hoping to see some of the womenfolk or children. There was nothing but the dark desert and Mustapha and the two other men who had eaten with us. They were all looking at me with expressions I could not fathom. I felt a long way from home.

182

For the next hour and a half I was subjected to a torrent of questions and speeches about Islam. It was shouted in my face, not angrily, but fanatically.

'Do you know the brotherhood? Do you know the path, the one path, the right path? Who is your mother, your father? Do you believe in me, in Mustapha? Do you?' and so on. My answers never seemed to satisfy and each time I hesitated out came, 'Who made the trees? Who made the animals? Who made the stars? Who even made the cigarettes you are smoking?'

'Marlboro' would not have been a good answer. Mustapha was serious, deadly serious. He shouted and jumped up and paced about, then he would be silent for a while, then he would come and sit beside me again and take my hand.

'Love,' he would say. 'Do you know love?' Gradually he became worked up again until I was forgotten and he was shouting to the sky, the trees, to everything, desperate, it seemed to me, to be understood, to share his faith. He bore down upon me, not giving me an inch, one minute asking me, the next telling me.

'The path, the golden path to where we all exist as one. Even now you are part of us. What will you do when you have to face Him, what will you say?'

And so the night went on and Mustapha became a man I had not seen in the boutique in town. In the darkness his sweaty face became all I could see. He filled the night. He was forceful, mad. Nothing I said could he understand. Always, 'Who made this? Who made that?' until I shut up. Sometimes, in a lull, I would see almost an apology on his face, embarrassment at the way he was treating his guest, but as soon as he started on any subject, he was away again. In the end he seemed very disappointed in me. I was not all he had thought I was. I was further from the path than he had imagined. In fact I was a very long way from the path, he said. He looked sad and when he had finished neither was I a happy man. The experience left me feeling strangely guilty. Had I in some way misled Mustapha? Did I deceive him by my mere presence in his country? Did the culture of the West, of which I was a representative, have any right to poke its nose into the culture of others and perhaps confuse and unleash something it did not understand?

The next day Mustapha was polite but cold. I had to find my own way back to town. When I saw him later, though, he invited me into his boutique for tea again.

'Hospitality is a great gift,' he said, 'to be given freely.' But it was not the same.

Later I met my soldier friend, all spruced up in a clean *bobo* instead of his army uniform of the day before. He was delighted to see me and told me he had met some good friends with whom he had passed the night. He was very nice to me because I was quiet that morning. This was Kiffa, the new Mauritania by the Road. I was in deeper water here, I thought to myself, as I waited for the Landrover for Tamchekket to prepare for departure.

16

Sal of Tamchekket

The old French fort of Tamchekket appeared at dusk on top of a
sand dune. It could have been a film set, especially in the grey light
of evening. It had ramparts and a limp flag at the top of a short,
square tower. Behind it lay the town like a collection of bricks left
in a sandpit, and behind the town was a forest of trees in a *oued*.
The trees were tall and well canopied and looked like a dark green
river winding across the desert plains.

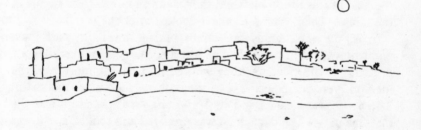

Sal was the name of the man I stayed with in Tamchekket. He
was a vet. My soldier friend from Kiffa was quite relieved when he
turned up at the police post where I was dropped off and whisked
me away to stay with him. He went off to the fort in a buzz of reunion

185

with his comrades-in-arms. Imprisoned there was an ex-president of Mauritania.

Sal lived in a yard with a family, not his family because he was only posted to Tamchekket. The yard was really just a part of the desert that lay outside the small house and the family was really only a sort of a family, because few of its members were related to one another. There was the mother whose husband had left her long ago, and her young daughter. There was a younger woman who had a boy of about six. She had no husband and was on the lookout for one. And in the corner of the yard lived a very old man and woman with their grandson, a shy teenager. Sal and his boss, the chief vet of Tamchekket, were the family providers and the chief vet acted as father. At the present time he was absent from the town.

They were a quiet family. During the whole time I stayed with them I never heard the old man and woman speak at all. The only times I had any reason to speak to them myself was when I needed to borrow the old woman's hand-mirror in order to have a shave. Even then she said nothing, just looked at me suspiciously and when I brought the mirror back, snatched it away from me as though I was a thief. Her husband was very old. He did not look as though he would be around for much longer. The two of them spent all morning and all night in their corner of the yard, only leaving it in the heat of the afternoon when they went into one of the rooms of the house. Their young grandson looked after them.

In fact the whole family passed most of their time in the yard. Each night they slept in it, in the late afternoons and evenings they sat in it and in the mornings they worked in it. In the mornings, the menfolk were not expected to be there; it was the women's domain. The house was cleaned and shut up. The yard was swept and the mats taken up. The day's food was prepared and cooked and it was only after midday that the men were expected to return.

There was a wooden dais in the yard and the mother spent most of her time on it. She made tea for Sal and me in the evenings, not joining in our conversations but watching us. Sometimes I thought she was not happy having me in the yard because of all the extra work it entailed: somehow I seemed to need twice as much water for washing and drinking as anyone else and it all had to come from the wells in the *oued* below the town. It was a long, hard walk with a bucket of water on your head. But she was a good, motherly woman and her smile when it came was as warm as a summer's eve. When I left Tamchekket she pressed a bag of dates into my hands.

Some people said that Tamchekket was not a good town to be in. It was just an administrative town for the regions round it. It had no history other than that it was built by the French, and the people were too poor to feed well all those who were posted there. Sal did not think this. He liked Tamchekket, or at least he was going to make the most of it. I also liked Tamchekket, but then I had not been posted there for three years.

The favourite time of day for me in Tamchekket was the very early morning. I used to sleep on a mattress outside in the yard and I would wake up each morning before the sun had risen. The others would still be asleep, curled up on mats with sheets pulled over their heads. There was a mongrel puppy that lived with the family. He already knew that his role in life was to be a guard dog and he tried hard, despite his age, to be a good one. Friends of the family would joke about him.

'I see you've got a new guard dog,' they would say. 'He looks very fierce!'

When I woke early in the mornings the puppy would be pattering about, disturbing the chickens and goats. Sometimes a sheep might wander over to the yard and the puppy would yap at it to keep it out, as any decent guard dog should. But most of the time the puppy was very bored. Then he would forget his role and try playing with the passing sheep, pouncing up and down and pawing the ground in front of them. The sheep would look at him as if he was mad. Sometimes he even tried playing with the yard cat, not a sensible thing to do as the cat was not very good-humoured and did not think much of the puppy's overtures. Generally it just gave a loud hiss but sometimes the puppy did not understand this warning and would yap and pounce, thinking he was in for a bit of fun. Then the cat would just lope away, leaving the puppy looking after it, puzzled.

What the cat did in those early hours was to chase insects in the air. Actually it looked rather foolish doing this, like someone trying to juggle but not getting on very well and going cross-eyed in the process. The chickens also chased the insects, scampering after crickets that sprang across the yard every time they came too close. But in their beady eyes they had determination and generally they caught the crickets in the end and pecked them to pieces before swallowing them. The few goats in the yard wandered about looking

for something to eat. Really anything would do: a piece of wood, a scrap of plastic, sometimes even clumps of their own fallen hair. They chewed pensively for a while and then went back to their wandering. Sometimes they would walk across my legs and attempt to nibble my sheet. Then I would wave a hand at them and they would scatter like startled pigeons. The puppy would look up at me in wonder, but he would not come over to try and play with me. He had learned the hard way, as all puppies do in Africa, the lesson that dogs do not play with humans.

As I watched the animals, the sky would turn orange and then gradually fade into blue, a sunset in reverse. The air would be cool and the day still silent but once the sun had risen and the tops of the houses were in bright sunlight, it would be the end of the early morning peace. The family would rise and the sun would begin its progress into the sky in earnest, soon turning the morning into a furnace, the afternoon into an oven and the evening into only a slight and reluctant release. Each day in Tamchekket was, climatically, an ordeal.

Sal was a very popular man in Tamchekket. He was a Hassan, a warrior as he put it, one of those 'of the gun', and most of his close friends were also Hassans. But he was also friends with many other people, in fact so many that it sometimes took him half an hour to walk a hundred yards for all the greetings he would have to go through. He was also very well respected in the town, even though he was still only a young man. The reason for this was not only that he took his job seriously and visited the mosque regularly but also because he cultivated respect. To begin with, he was one of the best-dressed men in town. His *bobos* were always startling bright and clean and his sandals well polished. He had a small goatee beard that he kept well trimmed and a fine set of shiny black whiskers that each morning and afternoon he combed meticulously, and which matched his shiny black eyes. And his general way of carrying himself and addressing people engendered respect. He held his chin high, his back straight and when he walked he did so with his hands held behind his back like the village elders. Sal was well educated and intelligent and he knew when and to whom to show respect – he never passed the elders of the mosque in the street without giving them a slight, deferential bow. And not least he was respected and liked so much because he was a good man; he thought of others all the time, he was over-generous and he was a fine upholder of the traditions of his faith and culture.

Sal and I became good friends. When he went to work in the mornings I would go with him. We would walk through the town and he would greet almost everybody we met on the way. Down in the *oued*, a little short of the veterinary office, was the place in which the cattle were butchered. Sal would stop off here to check the meat for disease, as was part of his job. He would slice open a piece and, seeing that it was healthy, get the butchers to send some up to the family in the yard.

Outside his office there would be a small collection of sick animals and their owners: a donkey with a woman, a baby goat with a boy, maybe a cow with a man. Sal had a helper who would be there already, the kind of man who would have made a good nurse in an eighteenth-century psychiatric ward. He wore a white apron and had huge, rough hands. Sal would take a look at the animals and then retire to his office while his helper pinned them down and stuck things into them. Sometimes the remedies would not work and Sal would be called out again when the animal seemed on the verge of death. Baby goats and sheep were the ones who mainly fell into this category. It was often hard to determine their illness and they died very easily.

Other than these odd jobs on the town's resident animals, this was a quiet time of year. Most of the animals, and indeed many of the people, were now out in the desert, making the most of the last of the grazing that had come with the rains. In a few months' time Sal and a small team of helpers would tour the desert camps, inoculating the livestock against disease, then in the height of the summer many of the herders would come back to the towns so that the rich merchants who owned many of the animals could feast on their milk and meat.

Even at this time of year, though, a vet's lot was not always an easy one. One morning, for example, the owner of a cow Sal had impounded because it had a contagious disease turned up. He was a tough, desert man, the kind who does not take kindly to the rules and regulations of others, the kind who would quite willingly lay his life down for the protection of the animals upon which his family depended. At first he was shy and a little nervous in front of Sal sitting behind the desk in his office in his smart clothes, but he was determined to get his cow back.

'Why,' he asked Sal, 'have you impounded my cow when there are so many others that have the same disease?'

He then hinted that it was some sort of prejudice. A row ensued. The desert man was incensed. He thought he was being wronged

190

and he forgot his nervousness and shouted loudly at Sal. But Sal was not a Hassan for nothing. He knew how to deal with these stubborn desert types. He shouted back, becoming quite fierce himself, and then announced that he was only doing his job but would take the matter to the police if the desert man felt an injustice had been done. The desert man left, still shouting. Sal smiled serenely, hitched up his *bobo*, and said that we would go to visit the chief of police. He closed up the office and we left.

The chief of police was a good man. He was big and hairy and we found him at home, surrounded by his large family. He took us to a room where he listened closely to Sal's story. Soon the desert man turned up and hunkered down in a corner, looking a little hunted in these unfamiliar urban surroundings. He told his story and the chief of police listened. Soon Sal and the desert man were arguing with each other again. The chief of police smiled knowingly, but was a little embarrassed, because he was a mild man himself. He could quite clearly see that the problem was not an easy one: there was some rivalry between the desert man and the essentially modern, urban Hassan. The desert man was not going to let his cattle be taken from him by a vet any more than he would by cattle rustlers. And yet Sal had to do the job he had been trained to do.

Without letting the desert man know, by speaking in French, the chief of police made Sal appreciate the delicacy of the situation, asking him to take into account the way these desert types feel about being ordered about by, to them, strangers. At first Sal would have nothing to do with this line of argument because to do so not only would be failing in his duty, but he was also a Hassan and he was not going to be defeated by someone of a lower caste. His dignity would not allow it. But eventually the chief of police got him to see it in a different way. As a compromise, it was agreed that the cow should stay in quarantine, but only for a week. Neither side was particularly happy with this, but the chief of police was the sort of man who makes it easy for his decisions to be accepted. Quite how he managed this, I do not know, since the whole time he was involved in the negotiations he had two young children climbing all over him as though he was a climbing frame. They pulled his ears and beard, they undid his buttons and pulled all his papers from his pockets. He put the papers back, did up his buttons, stroked their arms and patted their heads. They undid his buttons and pulled out the papers again, and so it went on, a continuing, gentle battle that did not seem to distract him from dealing with a situation that was far more complex than it seemed on the surface. It took a long time because he did not rush it. He was a very good chief of police.

After he had finished work for the day, usually not long after he had started at this time of year, Sal would go to the marketplace in the middle of town. Unlike most of the marketplaces I had come across so far, many of the boutiques in the marketplace of Tamchekket were owned by women. Tamchekket seemed to have more than its fair share of abandoned wives and divorcees, in fact it seemed to have more than its fair share of women. According to Sal, they outnumbered the men three to one and in Tamchekket many of these women went into business. Sal was a great favourite with them as he had a good sense of fun. His entry into the marketplace livened them up visibly. Even though he came each day at the same time, it was as though he was a returning hero. He would go round the women, joking and laughing with them; he would buy packets of biscuits and nuts and sugar and go inside one of their boutiques to have tea. Other people would drop in and before long the woman would have a small party in her boutique. He would have serious conversations with any of his Hassan friends who dropped in, he would tease and joke with the town scoundrels and humour the fools, but all the time playing slightly to the women. He was like a brother or son to them.

There was, for example, one woman who was the matriarch of the marketplace, a very large, well-perfumed lady with much jewellery and a handbag. She had a small, slightly upmarket boutique which sold things like mirrors, scents, cigarettes and torches. She also had a chair on which she sat outside her boutique, surrounded by a gaggle of cronies. Sal would always go to see her first. She would give him small presents and they would have secretive conversations together about goings-on in the town. Then there were the rich divorcees with whom he played games. One of these was a handsome, middle-aged woman, languid and powerful like a panther. According to Sal she had many camels and many lovers.

'When are you going to find me a decent man to marry?' she would ask him.

'I can't find a man who could manage you,' Sal would reply, laughing. 'You're too much and too old.'

'Ah, but I'm rich,' she would purr. 'Find me a good strong man who could manage me. I need a big man, I'm very fierce at night.'

And then Sal and any of his friends who were in the boutique would joke with her, making coarse comments about the number of children she had had and the fact that indeed she would need a big man. The woman loved this sort of talk and she would go on about how divorcees were much more preferable for a young man because they were so much more experienced.

Sal enjoyed his morning hours in the marketplace; he enjoyed being involved in the intrigues and intricacies of town life. His relationship with the fools and the madmen was as good as it was with the mosque elders and the chief of police. Our relationship was one of liking each other and of Sal's determination to do good by a stranger in town. A stranger should not be made to feel like a stranger and should receive the best hospitality it is in one's power to give, he told me. He went out of his way to do this. I was seldom on my own as I was almost continually in his company and he made sure that the food that was served in the yard by the family was the best his money could buy. It was just that, he continually apologised, he did not have enough at the moment to give me the degree of hospitality he would have liked. There was a problem with functionaries' wages not being forthcoming and also he had to send a lot of his money to his mother and younger brothers and sisters who lived in the south. Still, the family of the yard had a busy time while I was staying with them and they ate meat every day. Every lunchtime there would be liver and choice pieces of meat and in the evenings there was often chicken. Sal made sure my clothes were washed, lent me a shirt and a turban that he then refused to take back and generally made me as comfortable as circumstances permitted.

He and I had many long conversations. He wanted me to understand his country and his religion. He was very proud of them both.

'We are like one big family,' he would say. 'Everybody looks after each other.'

And he would always make comparisons with Europe. 'If a man was to turn up in a village there as you have here, would he be welcomed into people's houses? Would he receive the same hospitality as you do here? No, I think is the answer.' It was very plain to him which was better. It was obvious.

'Do we have stealing and violence here like you do in Europe?' he would ask. 'And can it be a good thing for a man to distort his mind with alcohol the way you do in Europe? God cannot want us to do that, can he?' Again, it was straightforward. He had a clear view of what he thought Europe was like.

'It is not natural, not good,' he would say. 'You cannot have good sheep and cows like we do here. You feed them strange things. They do not live only off the land. Strange chemicals. And their meat must always go through a factory and comes in tins or plastic. It cannot be right.'

I was not sure what to say about the fat and healthy cattle and sheep of England compared with the scrawny things that passed as cattle and sheep here. But I did explain to him about butchers' shops. He was very interested and surprised that such things existed in Europe. But then the young men in Mauritania were filled with bizarre impressions of Europe and not a little misinformation.

'In Europe, if a man has no money,' Sal might say to me, 'nobody will help him. He would die of starvation while the people around him were eating. There, each man takes his food on a dish of his own, doesn't he? Here we share from one platter. We share what we have with our brothers.'

Any subject we discussed – marriage, war, women – Sal was proud of the way his culture approached it. This was very refreshing for me. I had met too many young men in Africa for whom Western culture was preferable to their own. But there were some things that were difficult to explain. For example, how people could try living without religion, could try making their own decisions on right or wrong, and the existence of a priest – a good priest and a good man – but one who liked a drink.

'How can he be good,' asked Sal, 'if he abuses himself in such a way?'

The only subjects I could not really discuss with Sal were the more fundamental beliefs and actions of the Muslims. Then I found that Sal, like Mustapha of Kiffa, would soon revert to, 'Who made the trees, who made the stars, who made the animals?' and so on, putting a stop to the discussion. Logic was good but it should not be taken to its limits. The faith was strong and plain and should not be tampered with.

Sal was young and idealistic and content. He was happy to be in Tamchekket, surrounded by people all of whom he felt as close to as if they were his family. There was poverty, but only in the materialistic sense and the Muslims are not supposed to be materialists; at least Sal was not one. Who can grade poverty in people who are not materialistic? Sal did not crave the trappings of the West, he said; the only thing he wanted was a camera. It was the one thing he would allow me; I could not pay for any food, I could not do any work, but I could send him a camera when I returned home.

The days in Tamchekket passed very quickly in Sal's company. In the mornings there would be the veterinary office and the marketplace. In the afternoons we would go to the house in the yard to sit out the long, oven hours. Hassan friends of his would often join us. We would drink tea and eat rice and meat and his friends would question me about politics because it was not often they had the chance to talk to a Westerner. Then they would play cards together. I was not generally invited to join them. They played a fast, complicated game at which they were masters. They could not tell me the rules; they were just something you either knew or did not. The one time I did play they said to me afterwards, 'You're very bad at cards.'

In the evenings we would visit friends. Sal had a girlfriend, one of the women who had boutiques in town. She was big and powerful, too powerful and too tiring, Sal would say to me sometimes. He could not meet her in public, as that would be showing disrespect to the town's elders, so in the traditional fashion he would arrange a rendezvous with her in a friend's house. They would talk and giggle together as lovers do and we would have tea with their friends. Sometimes we would play a popular local board game. Sal always tried to cheat but he never got away with it. All the onlookers would see. Often the onlookers would become so involved with the game that they took it over and the moment you threw the dice they moved your pieces for you, not letting you have any say at all. When Sal was losing he would sit back and let them finish the game for him. The end was always quite hysterical with excitement.

Occasionally, in the early evenings, we would go and visit some of the camps in the plains near Tamchekket. Like the town, these camps seemed to be inhabited mostly by young women. When we arrived, the women would be in fine fettle, full of games and play. Sal was all right because he knew them and their games, but the stranger with him was as perfect for them as a fledgeling fallen into a nest of vipers. They crowded round him, laughing gaily, their eyes glinting with mischievousness.

There were the ones who were forthright: 'My tent is that one over there. You can find it in the dark, can't you? You don't even have to marry me.' There were the ones who were devious and clever and purred like cats, and there were the silent ones who did things with their deep eyes, who were probably playing the biggest game of all. They fired questions at the stranger with such rapidity that he became confused. They ragged and argued with each other about him, making sure he understood what they said. And they laughed and giggled and brushed his arms unintentionally and pressed themselves close to him, quite overwhelming him with their musky perfumes.

They had a lot of fun and Sal sat there laughing at his stranger, telling him not to take it so seriously. But the stranger was unconcerned whether to take it seriously or not. He felt as though he was a dish that had just been served up, or perhaps for such ladies merely an aperitif. They were pretty and they knew it and, as they so often said, there were very few men around. They were sweet and charming and in that gay, evening mood. When Sal and his stranger left the women followed them and danced about them like village girls round a maypole. And then it was night and they reluctantly turned back to their camp, and their merriment and arguing could be heard coming out of the darkness for a long time. That stranger decided that he liked the desert camps and would make a tour of them. It was time to move on.

17

Two tours on a camel

There is something delightful, wonderfully delightful, about being mounted high on a camel, a turban wrapped about your head, and stepping out across a desert. Strapped to the side of your camel is a full water *guerba* and a gun. Behind you is a bedroll and a cooking pot. You are talking to your guide who is perched on the bedroll behind you. He points to some dark undulations far away on the horizon across some sand seas and shimmering plains.

'Those hills,' he says, 'are forty kilometres away. Beyond them is a desert of sand and beyond that, two hundred kilometres from where we now stand, is my home town.'

Your destination is in fact only the hills forty kilometres away but your camel is eating up the distance so effortlessly and you are so high above the ground that you think to yourself – we have water, we have food, we have a good camel, why don't we just take that sandy desert and go to your home town?

That night, with my saddle sores and my aching body, I was glad that we were not going to 'take' the desert of sand. And because of my saddle sores and the general wear and tear of riding a camel, for the rest of my two tours I walked as much as I rode. It always seemed to be when I was thus positioned, plodding behind the camel, that we came across other desert men. They would be mounted high

199

and elegant on their camels, in blue flowing robes, and they would look down at me. It was only once, towards the end, that at last I came across some of these impressive figures when I was mounted. Then I greeted them to their faces, on their level, and they laughed heartily and greeted me back.

This was not a journey like my previous desert walk. My guide may again have been called Ahmed, Sidi Ahmed this time, and I might again have named my camel Jemel, Jemel II this time, but it was a much more leisurely tour among the desert camps and this time to my relief my guide spoke French.

Sidi Ahmed was an old soldier, hence the gun. He did not do much with it, only clean it a lot and take pot shots at birds. Only about twenty per cent of his cartridges went off and he never hit anything, but he would never go too far from his gun. One of Sidi Ahmed's fondest memories was of seeing General de Gaulle inspecting the troops on Independence Day, the day before Sidi Ahmed left the army. He thought de Gaulle the epitome of all that was strong, honest and true. Sidi Ahmed himself was not unlike that. He was a desert man, a tribal man, and I could not hope for a better guide. It was Sal who had introduced us and we had negotiated, over a number of days, a mutually agreeable price for him and his camel to take me on two tours in the desert.

Sidi Ahmed lived in one of the camps not far from Tamchekket. I went there on the way back from our first tour. It had been a hard last ride, each jolt of the camel jarring my frame as though my bones were a stack of loose bricks. His children came out to greet us. A young boy took hold of the camel, handling it and unloading it as though he were a man. A young girl quickly brushed down the mats under the tent and put out cushions, playing the role of mother. She mixed a large wooden bowl of curdled milk for us, adding special amounts of sugar, and handed her father the tea-making implements. The tent was open-sided with a pole in the middle and a stack of family possessions at one end in tin trunks, hanging on a wooden frame. They did not have very much, as everything had to be able to go on to a camel when they wished to move.

When the wind blew it was quite cool under the tent. It funnelled beneath and the tent strained like a kite against the ropes secured to long steel pegs driven into the hard earth. Sidi Ahmed had seven children: three girls, three boys and a baby. One of his sons was a policeman in Rosso in the south of the country; one was a merchant in Tamchekket and one was the young boy who had taken the camel. His three daughters were still at home, one a toddler, one a girl about to bloom into maturity and one a well-rounded figure sitting in the women's part of the tent by the family possessions, waiting for a husband. Sidi Ahmed could not have had it better: three daughters to look after him, and to bring him good dowries as they were good-looking girls; one son young enough to be still at home when he became very old; and two earning money, with families of their own.

Sidi Ahmed sat back when he got home. His middle daughter massaged his feet and picked out the minuscule cram-cram seeds that come part and parcel with the grasses after the rains. They are sharper than splinters and cruelly barbed, and bury themselves into any exposed flesh. His young son crouched near him, watching him with admiration in his eyes, waiting on his every word and action. While Sidi Ahmed was thus occupied and his son helped him to make some tea, he talked to his eldest daughter. She was looking after the baby as his wife was off in Tamchekket for the day, and she told him all that had been happening in his three days' absence. The youngest daughter, the toddler, meanwhile staggered about the tent, quite drunk with youth. She was naked and grey with dust and a day's worth of grime. Half her hair was shaved as a prevention against lice. She picked up and studied everything she came across, as children will, and popped most of them into her mouth as a final test – sand, Sidi Ahmed's shoes, a knife blade and the water from the bowl in which Sidi Ahmed and I had just washed our hands, which she drank, most of it running down over her large pot belly. Sidi Ahmed scolded her for this last thing so harshly that she ran to her eldest sister, whimpering, and eyed him with big, welling eyes that soon had her back by his side, leaning coyly against him, Sidi Ahmed petting her back to good humour and winding his fingers in what remained of her wild mop of hair.

They were mostly like this, the camps I visited on my tours: small patches of desert shaded by a tent under which were laid mats upon which families sat and so made a home. There were poorer families and richer ones. The richer families had larger tents made from sheep's wool. In them would be proper mattresses and a wealth of the finely decorated leather cushions the women made. They would have herds of cattle and goats and camels. The poorer families were often people who had only recently been freed from slavery. They were black and trying to survive on their own, their tents little more than scraps of material sewn together. They were mostly growing small patches of millet and had only a few scrawny goats. They had few mats, if any, and wore only the rags of clothes; and always there would be many flies. Sidi Ahmed liked to try and stop with the richer families – he did not think much of the ex-slaves; they were all right but only servants, he said, and rarely rich enough to provide decent hospitality. He was a desert man. The slaves might be legally free but no rules or laws of a government in a distant town could so quickly change what had always been. They would give us what they could and often go without themselves because of it.

Whichever camps we went to, though, we were always given the best of traditional desert hospitality. There would be the inevitable and many bowls of goat's, camel's or even sheep's milk, curdled and well sugared, which Sidi Ahmed was able to down in one go like a camel at the trough. When there were cattle there would be bowls of cow's milk, still warm and frothy from the udder, and more often than not a goat would be killed. It came to the stage when I knew that my arrival in a camp meant the imminent death of one of these doomed creatures. The beast would be hauled off like a sack and after a last bleat and gurgle as it had its throat slit, followed by a quick and expert skinning job and a brief boil in a pot, there it would be on a platter before me, and Sidi Ahmed would borrow my knife and cut off the best pieces for me to chew on. Later I would have to ask him for my knife back, as it had a habit of finding its way into his pocket.

Our first tour was not south but north, to the ruins of an ancient town called Aoudaghost in the Tegdaust Hills. In its time it had been capital of the old and powerful tribe of the Lemtuna, capital of the Sanhaja Federation of the Berbers, capital of the Almoravids and once it had been conquered by the empire of Ghana and become its vassal. It had been a caravan town and a large commercial centre inhabited by a luxurious society of urban Berbers and rich Arab merchants who traded in goods from Europe, the Near East and the Maghreb. Within four hundred years it had been destroyed eight times, each time rebuilt on top of its ruins.

We found a family camped outside the hills of Tegdaust, and approached their tent from the front: out of respect to old tradition, strangers do not arouse suspicion by approaching a tent from the side or from behind, as this was once a land where banditry and raiding were an integral part of survival. We were greeted and after a brief exchange of news, mattresses were laid on a sand dune beside the tent. We were fed with milk and tea and goat in the evening and early next morning we went to see Aoudaghost.

I am no archaeologist and for me, as for sightseers the world over, the sight one has come to see is only a part of the whole experience of the journey there and back. To me Aoudaghost was just what it appeared to be, a large hillock of rubble. In the rubble the outlines of streets could be traced. In the brief but deep excavations there were large houses with thick stone walls and sophisticated stonework decorations. There were little street-side drinking fountains and small squares with monuments in them. There were drinking troughs for animals and a large mosque, the most ancient one in Mauritania.

It was not until I climbed the hills above its ruins that the form began to take shape and to live. Here, firstly, was a long, wide canyon. Running off it was another, that opened out into a small plain circled by rocky hills. On the plain was the town of Aoudaghost. I imagined below me a much more fertile land. There were large *oueds* at the bottom of the two canyons, and many trees. The plain was covered with grasses and there were clusters of palms and even some ponds of water left after the rains. The many outlying villages were surrounded by plots of millet and browsing cattle and goats; nearer the town were large encampments of nomadic tribesmen with herds of camels. Leading directly south from the town, out of the canyon, was a well-trodden route and from the hills to the north a path picked its way down to the plain. It was down this path that the long camel caravans came from the Maghreb, passing, perhaps, Chinguetti and others of the caravan towns on their way. It was a long, hard journey and Aoudaghost, sitting in the protective arms of the hills, must have been a happy sight for the caravanners and camels alike. By now they must have been extremely weary and thirsty. They must also have been relieved, for the journey from the Maghreb was a dangerous one. Sometimes whole caravans just disappeared in the desert; in fact, whole armies had been known to disappear. There was much banditry and treachery in the desert and wells were easily missed. The route to the south was much less dangerous; even in times of warfare, somehow the trans-Saharan commerce was not disrupted.

Looking down I could see an Arab merchant just leaving the town by the southern route. He is dressed in a richly embroidered tunic with piles of turban on his head, sitting in an ox-drawn cart with an awning over it to shade him from the sun. Behind him is a long line of slaves carrying boxes of cloth and guns and glass beads on their heads, to be traded in the south. The town itself is humming with business. There are troops of spear-carrying soldiers and herds of sheep coming and going from it like ants to a nest. One can almost smell its famous cuisine and the figs and herbs and spices of the Maghreb. One cannot see, but one can imagine, the beauty of its fair-skinned Berber girls who so please the Arab merchants and the travellers. Yes, below me is a desert metropolis basking in the ease of being a middleman between the rich Maghreb and the rich kingdoms of black Africa; until its next war, that is.

The hills of Tegdaust in which Sidi Ahmed and I passed the afternoon had none of this. The canyon had a single deep well a long way from the single village of three stone houses. We rested there for the afternoon. The village's goats and sheep were browsing for the day in the desert with its sons. When the shadows became long and Sidi Ahmed went to look for Jemel II, who had broken his hobble and gone for a long walk, I went up to a cave in the hills above the village where the villagers told me there were some cave paintings. I had heard that there were some near Aoudaghost.

There are many cave paintings and engravings in the Sahara and North Africa, some of them dating back as far as 5000 BC. The history of the Sahara can be seen in the paintings. Some of the oldest ones show near-life-size elephants and rhinoceroses, and the people are hunters with spears in a green and fertile land. In the next stage there are domestic cattle and the people are pastoralists, then appear horse-drawn chariots, and next men on horses and ox-drawn carts. The last stage, and the least artistic, shows men on camels in what by now is desert. Then for some reason the cave painters disappear. Perhaps they were chased out by drought or by the men on camels, the desert tribes who, with the introduction of the camel to Africa at the beginning of the Christian era, became fierce and feared, for they had the mobility and self-sufficiency to enable them to use the Sahara as a retreat from which to prey upon those in the more fertile regions to the north and south.

One of the most remarkable things about the cave paintings, however, was not only their age and the story they told, but their beauty. Those cave painters were great and natural artists, something easily seen in the elegant, leaping form of an antelope or the slow, methodical movement of a herd of long-horned cattle.

The artists have disappeared and the Sahara is no longer the great fertile savannah it once was, roamed over by animals, including even elephant and rhinoceros. There are no more pastoralists, no more oxen and carts and no more horses. The trans-Saharan trade has died and with it its towns. Now there are even few nomads, and the great desert tribes who for so long could live with the desert were conquered by Europe. And so the desert changed, and is changing still, left to its own droughts. Look as I might, I could find no cave paintings in the hills above Aoudaghost. All I found was an inscription that read, 'Wilson Kagai, 1960'.

The second of my tours with Sidi Ahmed and Jemel II was a five-day trek to a town called Tintane, back on the Road. Our course was southeast and in each step of our journey there was change, change from the Sahara to the Sahel, from sand and gravel to sprouting grasslands and even clumps of flowers. There were *oueds* with dams and fields of millet. Later there were round mud huts with conical roofs, and then there was that sure sign of the West African savannah, the large, bulbous baobab tree. At first there were the camps of white Moors with their women dressed in black, their feet, hands and fingers dyed with the henna that grows locally, their faces and arms stained with dark blue indigo. The women would accept us into their tents with no fuss and hand us bowls of milk. Later the menfolk would begin to appear from the desert, riding on camels or walking at a fast pace, hot and thirsty from a trek to the wells or a morning spent with the browsing cattle and goats. At first they would be quiet and shy, then there would be tea and goat and soon they would get the measure of me and draw closer, and the questions would begin. Soon they would be laughing, for Sidi Ahmed was a good entertainer. There would be the story of how he had stalked a big black bird in a *oued* we came to and only one of his bullets fired and he missed, and how Jemel II had taken me for a gallop and Sidi Ahmed had chased after me, yelling at me to pull on the rope.

I had a turban given to me by Sal's girlfriend in Tamchekket. It was dyed indigo and strongly perfumed and the indigo ran down my face when I sweated, and stained my hands. The women would laugh because this was the height of fashion, they said.

Life in the camps began before dawn and ended shortly after dark. Everybody had their role to play, the boys out first thing with the goats, the young men with the cattle and camels to the wells and pastures, and the old men staying at the tent conducting family affairs and leading the five-times-daily prayers. All the women, from small girls to grannies, were mothers to their brothers and fathers. There was rarely a time when they were not employed in winding leather cords, sewing patches of tent, curdling the milk in stiff goatskins and pounding and preparing food. Girls of only five or six might have a baby sister strapped to their backs and already they would know what to do with it when it cried or choked. They already knew how to clean the rice and start a fire, and how to clean the cooking pot with sand. They were already little women, they were demure and respectful to their elders and would soon know all the ways of drying and preserving meat, curing a goat or a camel skin and preparing all the meals. The life of the tent, its organisation, transport and erection was the domain of the women. The animals were the domain of the men and the life of the camps revolved round the animals, their protection, their nourishment and health, their procreation, their killing and curing and eating. No part of an animal went to waste, from skin to the marrow of their bones, because the animals were all the camps had. Goats were meat on the hoof; sheep were for a superior and special meal; cattle were bred for their meat and milk; and the camels were for transport and only very rarely killed, as they represented a man's wealth.

Generally the families with whom Sidi Ahmed and I stayed the

night would set mats on the ground a little aside from their tents. They would give us cushions and come over to us to make us some tea. I used to enjoy sitting on our mats in the evenings and early mornings, watching the families and their animals preparing for, or finishing, the day. Small boys seemed to get the bulk of the work. They would milk the cows and goats and be sent after the difficult camels. Cautiously, they would steal up behind them, then more often than not, just as a child was within reach of the ring in a beast's nose, off the camel would trot with the boy scampering after it. Round and round the camp they would go until the camel was at last worn down by sheer perseverance.

The boys of the camp grew up very quickly, as did the girls, who by the age of fifteen or sixteen were large, full women, the larger the more desirable. Not so long ago, in order to produce a desirable daughter, a mother might force-feed her with milk each day. Sometimes this was taken to extremes and girls had been known to drown.

Many of the camps had chickens and always a dog or two. The chickens lived in cardboard boxes and were experts at making a living from the dust and scraps that lay about the tents, but the dogs did not have a good time. They were skinny, flea-ridden and limp, often kicked in the ribs for coming too close to the tents. Still, they were fiercely loyal to their homes. They were supposed to be a protection against the hyenas of which there were few, if any, left in this part of the Sahara.

Last thing in the evening all the menfolk would come over to Sidi Ahmed and they would stand in a line to say their prayers. Then they would leave us and Sidi Ahmed and I would talk for a while as the desert became dark. Before we slept Sidi Ahmed would try giving me his blanket in case I was cold. The one I had was his anyway, but he would want to give me the other one as well and say that he would be all right without one.

'But Sidi Ahmed,' I would say, 'I cannot have two and you none.' He seemed to think that I could.

With all the animals about, the nights, when they came, were rarely quiet. The cattle would be stamping and chewing the cud. The camels would be gurgling and groaning to themselves and padding about with their hobbles. The goats would be restless, rustling against each other, the rams snorting and chasing the young, flighty ewes; and the dogs would be barking at scents in the air and dashing after shadows. It could be like trying to sleep in a farmyard. In the mornings we would be off as soon as the sun came up. We would give tobacco and sugar and aspirins to the families and more often than not someone would have taken a fancy to one of my possessions, like a colourful handkerchief or a penknife, and would ask for it straight out.

One family with whom we passed an afternoon were as merry as a picnic in a summer's field. They did not draw breath from the moment I arrived to when I left. Their tent was below a rocky outcrop on a plain, patchworked with bare earth and swathes of yellow cram-cram grass. They had one son who could speak good French. He was a student in Nouakchott and was passing his three months' holiday drinking milk in the camps and getting away from it all. Actually, though, he was by now quite bored and missing his friends and his life in Nouakchott.

'Life in the desert is very hard,' he said.

'Yes,' I said. 'It must be very hard for them.'

'Oh, no,' he said. 'It is hard for people such as you and me who are used to a different life,' and he went on to tell me how in the summer it is sometimes so hot that it is difficult to do anything and how his family had to walk for two days to get water.

'But life is very good for them,' he said. 'They have their animals, their children and peace. They are very content. They stay in the desert all year round. Some families go to the towns in the hot season but not mine; they only go to buy sacks of rice and millet.' He was very proud of his family and their life in the desert.

One of the sons in the tent was deaf and dumb.

'My brother has two deaf-and-dumb friends,' my friend said, 'and the three of them know the desert like no one else and are the best men with camels.'

209

His brother sat watching us. He looked as well put together as anyone could be: small, strong and self-sufficient. He smiled at us and spoke to his brother by making signs with his hands and then he was off, up the rocky outcrop, bounding from boulder to boulder like a leopard. My friend watched him go.

'He knows the desert like no one else,' he said with pride.

Our first taste of the Sahel came on the third day in a wide valley planted with millet. Sidi Ahmed called it 'Mustapha's *oued*'; even though Mustapha was a poor Harratin, Sidi Ahmed had great respect for him because he was renowned for his good hospitality. Mustapha was big and gentle and blind. He had two wives and a large family with which he cultivated the valley each year after the rains. The crop of millet was bad this year because the locusts had eaten much of it.

'How can I stop the locusts from eating my millet?' Mustapha asked me, presuming that, being a Westerner, I must know such a thing. He said that there was an aeroplane in the district spraying the crops against the locusts. It had sprayed his valley the day before, but it did not seem to have killed the locusts. He said he did not like the aeroplane. He was scared of what its 'poison' might do to his valley and his family and animals. He hoped it would not come again.

After this strip of Sahel in Mustapha's valley there was a broken landscape of rubble with a track through it, then a pebbly plateau scattered with the shards of trees that looked as if they belonged to a World War I battlefield. Just how many of their deaths were the result of drought and how many of villagers' axes it was hard to tell, for few of the trees had escaped the cannibalisation that takes place throughout the Sahara for the purpose of collecting firewood. We rode across the plateau, Sidi Ahmed mounted on the back of Jemel II as always, and myself riding in front, steering to his directions.

To keep him at a trot we would have to devote all our attention to giving him a continual beating with a stick and our feet and making plenty of encouraging umphs and urrghs. Sometimes he would get fed up with this and stage a sit-down strike. Then, sadly, we would have to give him such a beating that he would at last stand up again. Camels are quite clumsy at the best of times, but when Jemel II was in this sort of mood he found it possible to trip over the smallest stone in our path. On one occasion, to his great consternation, a fly flew up Jemel II's nose. He flapped his nostrils and set up a great bellowing, but he was unable to dislodge the intruder. I really felt quite sorry for him, with two bullies on his back and a fly up his nose.

The beginning of the end of our journey was the valley of Tinkara, which we came across at the end of the plateau. The valley was over fifty kilometres long, very wide and ran all the way to Tintane on the Road, a long tentacle of the Sahel reaching into the desert: far below us was a savannah as beautiful and fertile as the gentle plains of East Africa. The green and yellowing grasses lay thick and tall and there were clumps of bushes and many large, spreading trees. Once Sidi Ahmed, Jemel II and I had picked our way down into the valley, there was no sign of any people. It was almost dark before we found our first camp.

The next day we passed the village of Tinkara, a village of Harratin. They were no longer about the traditional business of animal husbandry but had many large fields of millet. As we were passing them we heard the drone of an aircraft and then, far up the valley, we saw the spraying plane that Mustapha had spoken of, diving on some fields of millet as though they were an enemy.

At midday, when Sidi Ahmed and I were very tired and thirsty, we sought refuge in a village of Peul tribesmen. This was an African village with its walls of grass enclosing yards and round mud huts.

'This is a very bad place,' was one of the first things a young man said to me. 'Very boring, no music and no fun.' He went on to ask me about cigarette brands and Western popular songs. It was a different Africa. There was a small girl I noticed as I lay on a dais in one of the mud huts with Sidi Ahmed. She was sucking at a bird's head. The head was large and had a long beak and it was fresh, with feathers, eyes and all. She sucked at it all afternoon, like a lollipop, until there was only beak.

After this Peul village there was nothing but scrub until Tintane

211

and the Road. First there were no camps and then suddenly, beside the Road, there were more than I had seen in the whole of my tour. The only people we saw on the last day had been some men and boys herding a couple of thousand sheep. They were taking the sheep to their *patrons* in Tintane, who would sell them up the Road.

We camped that night with the herdsmen in a large clearing in the scrub. Each group of herdsmen built a fire and sat round it like cowboys, drinking tea and talking; I bought a sheep from them which was cooked and shared all round. For a long time after it became dark the groups of men shouted to each other from fire to fire, then the fires died down and the shouting became spasmodic. There would be questions and, five minutes later, an answer would come from the night. At last there would be just the odd statement and then

212

just the night and the herds of thousands of sheep, restless and circling round the sleeping camp.

In Tintane next day, after a last, long, hard walk, we came to the Road. There was a long *palmerie* all fenced in with only one path through it to the Road. Someone had put a wire across the path, five feet from the ground and as we could not get Jemel II under this, we had to make a three- or four-kilometre detour round the edge of the *palmerie*. We were so tired and thirsty, Sidi Ahmed and I, that we cursed the man who had put that wire there until we could only laugh. Then we stepped on to the neat grey surface of the Road. It was only a road and it was in the lands I had been walking and living in for the past few weeks, but everything felt different on the Road.

Sidi Ahmed had a relation in Tintane with whom we passed the afternoon, an old man who had come to live in Tintane a long time ago. He was a merchant and he sat on a dais watching the Road, taxis and trucks passing him now and again. I left Sidi Ahmed and the old man together.

18

A Peul village in the south

I was back on the Road, slightly aimless, unsure where to go next.
The Road was not unlike a river: not only did the lands in which
it lay shape themselves about it and drain into it and settle on its
banks, but also, like any big river, it had a powerful current. Not
surprisingly, this flowed towards the sea and so the flotsam and jetsam
that drained into it inevitably ended up being deposited on its delta,
in this case the town of Nouakchott. This had already happened to
me once before, as it had happened to so many others. This time,
though, I stirred myself enough from the lethargy of a taxi ride
towards Nouakchott, abandoned my ideas of a shower and comfort
and the friends in my hotel, and did what I call 'stepping out' –
breaking the routine of inevitability, like getting off a train at the
wrong stop.

I stepped out in Aleg, about halfway back to Nouakchott. At first
there was nothing new; the taxi park was the same as the one in
Nouakchott and Kiffa and all the roadside towns. But then I bought
a ticket for another taxi that was going to the far south of the country,
bordering the Senegal river. The passengers were not Moors. We
were heading to a more fertile, agricultural land mostly inhabited
by Mauritania's large minority of black African tribes. The passengers
did not stop talking for the entire journey and one man, just behind

215

my ear, gave an almost continuous monologue about the types of personal economy one could employ in order to be able to afford many children and, if possible, more than one wife. No one listened to him much.

The road was of tarmac at first and as straight as a road can be. Far ahead of us, shapes appeared on its glossy surface and slowly grew into trucks and other cars. The country was scrub, unexciting, empty scrub that did nothing until we were suddenly upon the river, and then it changed. The river was receding from its annual flood and it had lost its thread. Lakes and ponds and canals of floodwater spread out for five or ten kilometres either side. Crops were planted in the moist earth from which the water had drained away and this was the agriculture of the south. Along with the meagre produce of the desert and the harvest of imported and Aid-donated food which arrived at Nouakchott's port, it was the sustenance upon which Mauritanians survived.

The journey should have been very quick because of the speed at which our driver went, but there were so many police roadblocks in the south that it was not. There must have been ten blocks on the route we took and at each one we were delayed a long time as our passports, permissions and *laissez-passers* were checked. When we came to one of these roadblocks our driver stopped the car at quite a distance from it, then put the car into first gear and drove up very slowly. If one approached the block in second gear the policemen could become very angry. They got angry very easily because it was not pleasant having to sit in the ghastly heat beside the road all day. And it was not a good thing to make a policeman

angry, because if one looked close enough there was not a vehicle in Mauritania that was not in some way 'irregular' and could therefore attract a hefty fine. No, instead, one drove up to the roadblock in first gear, then wound down the window and greeted the policeman as though he was a long-lost brother. If you were lucky, one of the passengers might know the policeman or might just be of the same tribe. Then it would be all right, even if you had driven up in second gear, since the policeman would talk to the passenger, shake everyone else's hand and wave the car on its way. Sometimes the policemen were just bored. Then they might take you into their huts or tents and talk to you while they had some tea. Of course, this could be very irritating but one got into the spirit of it and smiled at the right times and learned to look appropriately impressed or concerned or even indignant. Drivers had to be very patient and it could help if they had a little loose change in their pockets. Unfortunately, the passenger in our car who was discussing his personal economy theories with such enthusiasm did not have good papers for travelling to the south. The repeated negotiations over this were often quite protracted.

Our destination was a town called Kaedi, capital of the southern province of Gorgol. On the way we passed a few villages of Peul tribesmen with big, ornate mosques painted in bright pinks and sky blues like birthday cakes. One village had only about ten houses and three of these were mosques.

In Kaedi the taxi stopped and everyone got out and started to disappear. No, there was nowhere to stay in Kaedi, I was informed. It was hot and the town was modern and scrappy and I did not know what to do next. In my taxi there had been a Peul man with whom I had talked. He was quiet and friendly and had told me he was an accountant for a French mining company in Nouadhibou, going home to his village on compassionate leave because his newborn son had recently died. Seeing that I was at a bit of a loss in the taxi park, he asked me whether I wished to come and stay with him in his village. I thanked him and said I should like to very much. His name was Mohamadu.

We picked up another taxi almost immediately and it took us about an hour to get to his village along the dirt piste that runs through the far south of Mauritania. As we drew nearer to it Mohamadu became increasingly excited.

'Ah, the rains were good this year. It has not rained properly for fourteen years, but look at all that water,' he said, indicating some lakes a long way off to the south, that looked like mirages.

'The crops will be good this year and my people will be very happy,' he said. Then he saw an old lady walking along the road with a basket on her head.

'My aunt, my aunt,' Mohamadu cried, 'that's my aunt.'

After this he became quiet. He was clearly nervous, for he had not been home for eighteen months. When we arrived in Leqceiba, his village, Mohamadu took a newly washed *bobo* from his small bag and put it over his Western clothes beside the road. He combed his hair and brushed the dust from his shoes and with these alterations his appearance changed dramatically. Instead of being the young, Westernised man I had thought, he became an older man with flecks of grey that I now noticed in his hair, and the dignity and bearing of a village elder.

The village was very big. It was brown from the earth from which it was shaped; a warren of alleyways and tall, smooth walls and family yards and tin-roofed homes. Mohamadu exclaimed that indeed it was now more like a town and had considerably increased in size even since he was last here. The Peul were traditionally pastoralists, semi-nomadic cattle herders. Their large herds of white, long-horned cattle had been to them the epitome of all that is meaningful in life, as camels are to the desert nomads. The droughts of the 'seventies and early 'eighties had hit the Peul hard, because they lived mainly in the Sahel which had been a very badly affected area. Many of the families, such as Mohamadu's, had lost all their cattle and so had had to take up agriculture instead. They had settled in villages such as this, and day by day more Peul were doing the same.

As we drew nearer to the part of the village where Mohamadu's family lived, we began to come across people he knew. They would greet him but not detain him, for he was a son returning to his home.

218

They would fall in behind us with the trail of children who were already our entourage. Before long we had a large crowd hurrying with us through the alleyways, Mohamadu at its head, looking apprehensive.

Then, suddenly, we turned a corner and were in a very large yard surrounded by small huts like a village all on its own. People were coming at us from all sides and then we were engulfed in noise and commotion and the forms of fifty or so relatives. There were faces all around us, smiling and lit up like moons, but this was no Latin orgy. There were no great hugs and wailing and tears. A certain reserve was maintained – just. There were misty eyes and pounding breasts, and the women fluttered about.

'Mohamadu is home, Mohamadu is home,' they exclaimed again and again. Twenty or thirty children of every shape and size shook our hands, then hovered about, looking serious and important. Young men gave Mohamadu a brief embrace and then stood by his side like awkward sentinels. It was like the official reception of an explorer after a long and hard expedition, but the air here was thick with unspoken emotion and Mohamadu looked peaked and moved. Soon we were drawn over to some comfortable mattresses that had quickly been laid out in the yard. We sat down and more and more people arrived, as the news of Mohamadu's return spread through his family's part of the village. Each one shook his hand and then mine, then quickly sat down before us. Mohamadu's head was lowered as he muttered the ritual greetings.

'Abaraka, abaraka,' he said, and when old people came he stood up and bowed his head and everybody said, 'Abaraka, abaraka,' and all the other words of greeting. This went on for a long time. No questions were asked, nothing was said, apart from the code of greeting that everybody muttered like a prayer. Even when Mohamadu's wife brought us a bowl of milk there was no exchange of news – only a polite and brief greeting. At our feet was a mat of children, pressed tight and frisky, and around us the crowd grew.

Bowls of milk were produced and still Mohamadu said 'Abaraka, abaraka,' staring at his feet as if too moved to look up. Then a little

219

girl, as beautiful and delicate as a newborn foal, wormed her way round the side of a doorway nearby. Her thumb was in her mouth and she rubbed herself coyly against the doorframe. She eyed Mohamadu with eyes that were deep and hurt and when he called her over to him they brimmed over with tears and she drew back. Some of the young men laughed gently and tried to encourage her from where she stood, but she shook her head and cried because she was shy, because Mohamadu was her father and she had not seen him for a long time. Then, when the attention was off her and she thought she had been forgotten, she trotted over to him. Then she was clinging to him, her head pressed against his chest, her eyes fixed and distant. Mohamadu said nothing, just stroked her hair. She did not leave him until much later when she fell asleep and was gently lifted from his lap by her mother.

We did not move from those mattresses until well after midnight. The family, or at least many of its members, sat around us, staying close to Mohamadu. They surrounded him with his people. He was quiet for most of the time and they let him be quiet. They asked no questions but just made merry, laughing and joking and fooling around. They let him join in as he wished and they let him sit quietly with his grief for his lost son that now, in the heart of his family, was free to come to the fore.

Many different kinds of millet dishes were produced – each branch of the family sent Mohamadu food, as they were to for the next few days: millet with beans and a sauce made from the leaves of beans; millet with milk and pieces of fish; millet on its own, or spiced; millet always a little different, but always millet, for millet was all they had. We crowded round the bowls of food and ate to the light of a moon that had come up over the walls of the houses across the yard and the night became cosy and warm in the heart of an extended and close-knit family rallying at a time of sadness because one of its sons had died, and of joy because one of its sons had returned. As the children dropped off to sleep they were picked up one by one and put in a line on the ground and a blanket was thrown over them, small and big ones alike. Mohamadu's daughter stole back to him

220

again and slept in his arms. When the night grew deep, mosquito nets went up outside the houses round the yard as each part of the family went to bed. Soon the yard was filled with these ghostly shapes illuminated in the dim moonlight. Mohamadu showed me to a small open space where I could sleep behind one of the houses, where there was a mattress and a mosquito net.

The next day the yard and its houses and people looked good in the early morning light. Mohamadu's mother, with a kind face and strong arms, was milking the only cow the family had left in the middle of the yard. Outside their door each part of the family was making chicory coffee and women were going to the wells to collect the day's water. They wore dresses of batik with colourful designs and out in the town there were little coveys of them coming and going to the wells, large ladies with big enamel bowls on their heads, smaller ones with buckets and young girls with saucepans. Once the cow was milked, she was sent off with a herdsman and all the other town cows to browse for the day in the scrub. In the evening the herd of town cows and the town sheep and goats were left on the fringes of the town and made their own way back through the alleyways to their separate houses, like people going home after work.

After I had drunk coffee with Mohamadu and his family he said, 'Today it will be hot, so we shall stay indoors.'

And so we did, not moving from the house until dusk. As the day developed outside, the thick earth walls absorbed the heat and soon became hot to the touch, but inside it remained cool like a larder. In the evening the walls began to shed the heat and the house became like an oven. Then everybody moved their mats and themselves into the yard. Throughout the day the family stayed close to Mohamadu. They sat with us in his house and we did nothing but eat the many dishes of millet that were sent and watch the children at play. Mohamadu seemed quite content, in fact he seemed to need to sit and do nothing but be surrounded by his family and their children, to absorb some warmth like the walls of the house.

Mohamadu was a serious man. He had a good education and much responsibility. He had been sent to school in Kaedi and had then joined the French mining company for which he still worked and which had sent him to France for a year's training. Now he was in a good wage-earning job and that was a privileged position to be in, as there were not many such in the country. He had a great deal of responsibility, too, because only he and one of his brothers, who also had a good education and a wage-earning job, were in a position to support their large extended family: other than their fields of millet and their cow, the family depended on the money that Mohamadu and his brother sent them. It was he and one brother who had been educated. His other brothers knew only the Koran and the cultivation of their fields. Mohamadu had to live in Nouadhibou with his wife and children, but they had come back to the village a few months ago on the death of the baby. He worked hard, very hard, he said. So hard, in fact, that his life was devoted to his work.

At this time of year there was not much work to do in the fields; the crops had already been planted and were just waiting to grow. Every two or three days one of the elder boys would load up a donkey with water and food and, taking a younger brother with him, would go out to the fields. These were quite a long way away but once there they would replace whoever they found and do the job of scaring away birds and guarding the crop. They would come back a few days later when they, in their turn, were relieved of their duty. Other than this the menfolk had nothing to do at this time of year. They sat with Mohamadu and me and together we sweated in the intense heat and watched the children playing.

The children were the family's wealth, their joy and their diversion. Live revolved round them. It was like a continuous marvelling at the miracle of growing life. When the heat and boredom of the long days had made everybody else dumb and lethargic, the children remained filled with enthusiasm, with cheerfulness and squabbles and inventive play. The toddlers swaggered about experimenting with life, full of curiosity and hope. Small girls would play mamma, learning to balance cups on their heads and strapping shoes to their backs in place of babies. They would go up and down the yard, ordering their brothers to stand here or there and be a tree upon

222

which they could hang their washing. They would bully the baby goats and form gangs and gossip as the women do.

The boys, when they were at home, did not play. They sat with their elder brothers and were quiet and respectful as they were expected to be. It was in the village public spaces that the boys went to play. This was no-man's-land, out of the family sphere. There they got together with their gangs and lounged about on street corners like alleyboys. They would be full of games and mischief and quite ready, when a stranger such as myself came along, to have a bit of fun at his expense. In the evenings one of the family elders would give them their Koranic lessons and they would sit in a circle round a fire, chanting the scriptures they had painted on their wooden boards. They did not necessarily know the meaning of what they were chanting, could not even necessarily read Arabic script, but they learnt how to recognise the scriptures and to say them by heart and the more somebody knew the more he was respected and the more religious merit he had. The grey-bearded elder would throw dried grass on to the fire so they could see by the flames and they and their horseshoe boards would be silhouetted against the light. Some of the boys went to the village primary school and even some of the girls, but not everybody went to it and only a few of those who did would graduate to school in Kaedi.

I spent four days with Mohamadu and his family. They were not an easy four days. Most of the time was spent sitting in a house, sweating and itching with boredom and inactivity. It seemed that Mohamadu could not shake off his despondency. He was tired, very tired, he said. His wife was not. She was a pillar of strength, as indeed were all the women of the family. She was strong and handsome with the same depth of beauty in her eyes as her daughter. She was cheerful, as if nothing could get her down. In the depth of the afternoon, when the eating had been done and the tea had been drunk and there was nothing left to do but face the heat, when everyone else had sagged and slumped against the walls with minds numb with inactivity and the flies were causing a nuisance that one could not be bothered to stop, she would tell jokes and laugh at them herself

223

and her face would look determined and shiny with sweat. When the children became quarrelsome and a nuisance it was she who smacked them and then cuddled them to sleep. And when some water was needed or a hot coal for a fire, it was she who would get up and brave the burning yard to fetch it. It was she and the womenfolk who came into the house who chatted and laughed and kept us all human, for the young men had no work to do and no hope of much change in their life, and Mohamadu had the weight of the world on his shoulders and only his daughter could divert him.

In the evenings Mohamadu and I would go on a promenade to shake the idleness from our limbs. Often a cousin of his called Bull would come with us. Bull was large and well educated. Mohamadu said that he did not do anything with his education because he was very lazy, nor could he work in the fields because, according to Mohamadu, he was too fat. Despite this he was a leading member of the family and greatly liked, especially by the children, who used him as a teddy bear. We would do the rounds of Mohamadu's friends and relations. Most of the relations we went to see were old men or women sitting in the dust in their own yards on pieces of cloth. We would sit down close to them for a while and Mohamadu would ask after their health and thank God many times. One of his friends we went to see was a man like himself, working in Nouadhibou with a large family to support back in the village. We sat with him for an hour and a half, and not more than ten sentences could have been said.

One day we went to see the village *marabout*. He was a very old man, all fading eyes and grey stubble and beard. He was sitting on a small prayer mat next to a copy of the Koran and a large alarm clock. He proceeded, without hindrance, to give me a lecture on the Islamic faith. This was a gentle lecture, though. He often smiled and he spoke to a place somewhere at his feet, not into my face.

'Life is like a field,' Mohamadu translated to me, 'one of God's fields that we have been sent to work. Death is another of his fields and we should not be scared of the day we are called to that.'

Mohamadu translated every word the old man said, only now and

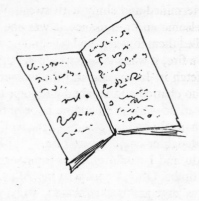

again getting a bit behind, but when he caught my eye and we smiled at each other he knew I did not mind if he jumped a bit.

'We have three important things that God has given to us,' the old man said, 'sight, hearing and the faith. Hearing is the most important because the man who listens well is a good and humble man.'

I heard the old man all right. There was no 'Who made the trees, who made the stars' with him. All he asked of people was that they listen to him for a while. And so I did, for about an hour and a half, and then I shook hands with him and we left.

Mohamadu was a deeply religious man, a good Muslim. Like his brothers, he had been brought up on a strict diet of religion and loyalty to the family and the faith. And, like his brothers, this upbringing had taught him to be humble and to do no evil to other men. By all appearances Mohamadu and his family were indeed humble and few thoughts of evil crossed their minds. They accepted the ill fortune that had taken their cattle and their proud lifestyle from them and they thanked God all the more for what they had, bringing their

225

children up as best they could to respect life and the faith. But Mohamadu had a hard path to tread. For him it was not merely a matter of accepting and cultivating the fields. He was educated, he had seen France and lived in Nouadhibou, far to the north. He saw things and understood things that his brothers did not. And what he saw was the suppression of his people, their consequent poverty and their hopeless plight.

One evening, as we walked back to the village after a stroll in the plains outside, he told me many things and he was angry. He told me how the Moors neglected to develop many parts of the far, fertile south. How the south had the potential to feed the whole country, but how the Moors would not like this because it would make the black African tribes of the south richer, more powerful. It was the black Africans who had staged the recent attempted *coup d'état* that had resulted in its leaders being shot. The Moors were afraid of the black Africans, Mohamadu said, because their numbers were catching up with those of the Moors in Mauritania. Not that that was the official case – they were still a small minority was what was said.

'Do you see any irrigation projects in this town?' Mohamadu said. 'Do you see any fruit trees or plantations? Why have we only ten wells and why is it that the Road was built to the north and not down here where the economic strength should lie? Why is it that my brothers and children will find it so hard to get an education and, if they do, why will it be nearly impossible for them to find a wage-earning job? Look at this town. Why is it so desperately poor, when a few kilometres away there is a vast supply of water? The answer to all these questions is easy. Because the Moors wish us to remain poor, uneducated and without any hope. They do not want the balance to be disturbed for they are growing powerful and rich on all the Aid that this country receives and they can set up their boutiques among those whom they keep poor and sell us that Aid food and they can use the Aid money to develop their Road and their towns and their agricultural projects on our land. We are too scared to complain because there might be a massacre. As it is, it is dangerous for us to promote our language and our culture. Our intellectuals

226

go to prison and mysteriously die. Yes, we are scared, and we can only wait.'

Quiet, gentle Mohamadu was not so quiet and gentle when it came to the age-old conflict of Bantu black Africa meeting Arabised north, a conflict that has become all the more complex and poignant with the concept of 'nation' and with the drought and the outside Aid that comes with drought.

The long wait continued that evening as it did every evening. We sat on mats in the yard, very tired after a long day of nothing to do. There were more dishes of millet and tea, then I looked at the stars for an hour or so. They were nearly as good here as they had been in the desert. In one hour I counted eleven satellites and fourteen meteorites. When the moon rose later it washed out the stars, putting a coarse and blunt end to their play. At times like this I did not like the moon, although usually on dark African nights she was my friend.

The next day I left the village, sitting for an hour or two beside the road waiting for a minibus. In front of me I watched a group of young and naked children playing in the dirt. When one of them started wailing the grime and snot on her face congealed and the flies came for a feast. She sat in the middle of the road, clutching the end of a piece of discarded dirty plastic and wailing as if the world had come to an end. The other children and the people nearby ignored her. It was just too hot and too dusty and too much effort to do anything about her. After a while she put the end of the scrap of plastic in her mouth and rocked herself back and forth. I sat and sweated and felt sad to be leaving Mohamadu, and sad because I wanted to leave.

19

On a donkey

Morguel was only eighteen kilometres north of the Peul village but there I was back amongst the Moors. Where the Peul village had been huddled together like a termites' nest, this small Moorish town was spread out as if its inhabitants suffered from claustrophobia. There was a wide market street surrounded by a fragmentation of the square cement boxes that the Moors, when they are not in the desert, live in as if they were. Around it were rolling grasslands the palest greens, as if the verdure had been sucked from them, and run through with trails and wisps of sand that here and there collected into dunes.

I was left at dusk at the police post by the minibus that had brought me to the town. The solitary policeman on duty was small, swarthy and had very red eyes in one of those unfortunate faces that, no matter what, just look untrustworthy. Despite this and despite the fact that he was one of the breed of men who so trouble travellers at roadblocks, he was not a bad man. True, he availed himself of the opportunity of the arrival of the minibus to procure a new set of torch batteries, and true, he considerably delayed it as he chatted up one of the female passengers; but he took me under his wing, put me up for the night in the police post and helped me sort out my immediate plans for the future with enthusiasm.

My immediate plans were, as usual, uncertain, but they focused vaguely on a desire once again to take to the countryside, preferably with a beast of burden. Quite contrary to what I expected, the policeman did not view this idea with either suspicion, although he did study my passport for a *very* long time, or incredulity at the pointlessness of it. No, he thought it an admirable idea and would, he vowed, help me fulfil it the next day.

The following morning I was woken before dawn by my friend sweeping out the guardroom and the verandah upon which I was lying. He then straightened his crumpled uniform, clipped his revolver back on to his belt, tried in vain to organise his hair and told me that I would shortly have to make myself scarce, as the captain was coming to inspect the post. As I was hastily packing up my things he went back into the guardroom to appear again with the national flag, which he bore before him, neatly wrapped up, on the upturned palms of his hands as though it were a holy relic. Very slowly and with great dignity he made his way over to the flagpole in front of the police post and tied it on in readiness for the flag-raising ceremony. Shortly after, the captain arrived, and once we had stood to attention as the flag was raised I made myself scarce and went into town.

During the course of that day I became a familiar figure to the people of Morguel. The police post being out of bounds, I passed most of the day hanging around the market street, having tea with merchants and being questioned by curious women and young men. Everybody knew what I was doing in Morguel. They had heard about it on their radios. Ever since National Tourist Day a few months earlier, tourist had been a word that often cropped up; nobody knew quite what a tourist did but presumably I was the first of many to come. One old merchant with whom I had tea told me he had heard all about my mission and that it must be very hard. There was a general rallying round to help, led by my policeman friend. At one point I was on the verge of getting a camel, at another I was told that a horse had actually been sent for; but eventually it boiled down to a donkey. This was a new experience for me but the donkey, as donkeys do, looked very sweet with its big, funnel ears and dainty feet. The guide who was procured along with it looked very proud and richer than guides generally do.

We left Morguel in the middle of the afternoon. My guide, who was called Essmou and who in town had been silent and serious, now became quite jolly. He was a neatly presented man with a goatee beard and a beautiful sky-blue *bobo*. He sat cross-legged on the donkey's back, his hand resting on the end of a stick and his bared head held high, as though he were a landowner making a tour of his estates. 'This is my country,' he said to me, 'and I am known by all the people in it.' He was a Hassan.

After a short while Essmou dismounted and I got on the donkey in his place. At first I felt rather foolish, jogging along with my feet a mere few inches from the ground; a different story indeed to being mounted high on a camel. But soon I was enjoying it. The afternoon was soothing into evening, a man was trotting beside me on another donkey chatting to Essmou, who walked a little ahead, and it felt good to be on the move.

My honeymoon did not last long. When we came to our first *oued* I was told to hang on tightly. I did, but as we descended the steep side of it, I, the saddle upon which I sat, the sack beneath it, and the baggage strapped all around, slipped to the side and with a thump we landed on the ground. The donkey turned his head to give me a look of deepest unconcern. From then on my relationship with the donkey deteriorated: in fact in a very short time I was cured of the desire ever to ride one again. To begin with, despite a donkey's size the mere operation of mounting is not easy if it has baggage strapped either side, as mine did. You have either to fling yourself at the saddle cowboy-style and hope that as you leap your leg clears the wooden promontory that sticks out of it at the back, or you have to go through the very undignified process of getting one leg up and then sort of lying half-across the saddle, hopping on the other leg, trying to right yourself in the middle. The first looks very impressive when it works but can be very dangerous if you catch, as I did, a very sensitive part of your anatomy on the way over. The second is much safer but best not attempted when there are too many people watching.

Finally installing yourself with your legs almost spread-eagled across the breadth of baggage is by no means a positive indication that you are going anywhere. Donkeys have an enormous capacity for standing stock-still and no amount of bashing will necessarily budge them an inch. They have developed, no doubt from centuries of being beaten by man, an incredibly tough hide, quite like the arms of an old armchair. You have to beat the beast, not with the sort of flimsy stick you might use on a more sensible animal, but with a veritable cosh. With this you deliver a blow that would kill a man and still sometimes the donkey will not move, but will instead turn his head to give you a look that makes you feel as insignificant as a fly. Then, sadly, you are forced into a sort of frenzied attack that leaves you feeling quite sick and angry, since it is quite likely you started out the proceedings a sane and pleasant chap.

These are all problems that anybody can have with a donkey and if these had been the extent of my problems with Essmou's beast I could quite easily have accepted it. Sadly, though, the situation was far more serious. This particular donkey seemed to have a particular dislike for the particular European who had paid to ride on its back. Somebody, according to Essmou, had to ride the donkey, as solitary donkeys travel best when they are ridden. I wanted to be that person at least some of the time because, after all, that is what I had paid for. The trouble was that when I was on the donkey's back, and when and if by some chance we were actually moving, we did so at an agonizingly slow pace. And then when Essmou, as he frequently did, went off for a short while to say a prayer or to talk to a passing traveller or some such thing, the donkey would, without delay, make for the nearest tree and stop stock-still in its shade, quite ignoring anything I could do. So there I would have to sit, defeated and foolish, until Essmou, in his own good time, finished whatever he was about and came over to give me a hand. He, of course, would not so much as lift a finger, just click his tongue a couple of times and the donkey would obligingly move on.

Generally, after an hour or so of this, I would lose patience and dismount, preferring to walk. Essmou would mount instead and instruct me to walk ahead in what he said was the correct place, for a solitary donkey likes to have something to follow. Clippety clop, I would hear. The merry sound of the trot would be as someone laughing behind my back. And when Essmou, as he was in the habit of doing, called to me, 'He's going well today, very fast, very good,' it only made matters worse. It was not as if I had not tried everything – cajoling with kind words and little pats on the neck, coaxing with chirrups and peeps as Essmou did, and then resorting to the ghastly business of a thrashing – but it was all to no avail, so generally the order of march would be Essmou mounted in his beautiful blue *bobo*, looking cheery and comfortable, and me trudging ahead thinking evil thoughts of the whole donkey race and convincing myself that Essmou and his donkey were in fact in league to humiliate and infuriate me as much as possible. When we passed through villages I was sure I caught the cruel tinkle of laughter and could imagine the villagers whispering to each other as they laughed. 'Look, look what that clever man Essmou has done. Not only has he got one of those tourists to pay for him to make a tour of his country, but also he rides the donkey and makes the tourist walk in front.'

We were going to a place called Batha. I never discovered how far away it was, for with Essmou any specific distance from, say, one village to another, was invariably fifteen kilometres, and any long distance was just 'very, very far'. The land we walked in was the same sparse grassland that lay about Morguel, interspersed with long stretches of black gravel. For a while there would be no people at all, then suddenly we would come to an area where there were many, living peasant lives centred round wells and fields of millet. Wherever there was the bed of a *oued* it would be planted with millet; down this far south it was nearly ripe. Near each *oued* there were camps of Harratin and beside each field sat groups of women and girls whose job it was to frighten off the small birds that spun from bush to tree and tree to bush, squabbling and from time to time nibbling at the millet seeds. There were men with hoes and hands as tough as bark, round straw hats on their heads; boys with bare feet as flat and cracked as camels' pads, faces fresh and alert and as filled with wonder and

surprise at the sight of us as those of their flocks of goats. We would meet families following the winding, sandy tracks with lines of donkeys, babies and grannies and the poles of their tents on the donkeys' backs. There would be fathers with sons, or wives with daughters, making trips to the nearest market town leading donkeys laden with grain. And there would be holy men walking alone, white skullcaps on their heads, prayer beads twiddling at their thumbs; and other men, like Essmou, making gentle tours from one centre of commerce to another on donkeys. Now and again herds of camels would appear a way off in the brush, a couple of turbaned men mounted on two of them, passing quietly and strangely detached through these Sahelian lands. At one time we came across two young Malian men in Western clothes, suitcases on their heads, making a long and illegal journey by foot from Mali to the desert mines of Zouerat in the north. They were very grateful for the water we gave them to drink.

At one well we came to a boy watering his goats. He had about fifty of them and he was only about eight, and all he had was a small plastic sheet crumpled into the shape of a bowl. He was having the greatest of difficulty in keeping the goats back and drawing water at the same time. Each time he poured the water into his sheet and turned to draw some more, the goats rushed at it and spilt it in their haste. He threw stones at them to keep them at bay but it looked as though he would be there for a good part of the day. At another well there was a crowd of Peul women filling a barrel and many buckets and bowls. Essmou did not want to wait for them to finish, as the water was very deep and there was not much of it anyway. But the women were surly, absorbed in their sweaty work, and told him to wait his turn.

'Since when has a man' (and a Hassan at that, not that Essmou said as much), 'had to wait to fill a *guerba* while some village women occupy the wells for so long?' he asked. But the women ignored him and it was only when he had stood meekly aside for a little while that they let him get at the well, and even then they made him draw the water himself.

Although the land sometimes gave the impression of being well watered, it was in fact as dry as a bone, for the rains had continued to be very bad. In a few months' time it would be scorched down to the bare earth, only the stumpy, badly hacked trees and the thorny bushes left.

'Is there no water?' Essmou would say, using the interrogative, as was his habit when he wished to tell me something.

'Are the rains very bad? Are there very few wells?' he would say.

We stayed our first night in a camp of white Moors who were friends of Essmou; they had five tents, three made from brown sheep's wool, the labour of the women, and two inferior white ones made from the coarse material that comes from Mali. In their presence Essmou was again serious and quiet and paid me very little attention: he did not want his friends to think he was a guide in any subservient sense. The only time that he laughed was when I mentioned that I had recently passed some days in a Peul village. Then he sniggered as if it was the most amusing of things. I slept badly that night, assaulted by insects and snuffling sheep, and the next morning everybody looked solemn and tired as if they too had had a bad night.

That morning the donkey went well (that is to say, at a steady, if painfully slow pace). At midday we came to a village of many round huts in a windswept, barren place. There was a tiny school room in which were squeezed thirty or forty children like mice in a hole. When I peered in the door, thirty or forty pairs of eyes, standing out of the dim light, stared back at me, unblinking and wide. Their teacher was a well-educated Moor who lived in a tiny mud hut beside the school with a mattress, and a sack of chalk and chalk boards for his pupils. When school ended he lined his pupils up outside and had them sing the national anthem and say some prayers. Then they were scampering off in every direction and soon they were swallowed up by the round mud huts and the village looked as deserted and barren as when we had arrived.

We passed the afternoon with the teacher and the village chief in the teacher's hut. The chief was as old as his wrinkled frame indicated. He said his village was many centuries old and that his people, who were Harratin, had been free men for longer than he could tell. But the village had no well, he said, only a water hole filled with hundreds of toads. The water from it, as I discovered after a long draught, was putrid and, to me, undrinkable.

'Where can we dig a well?' the chief asked me as I gagged. 'We have dug already in many places but never do we find water, although we know it is there somewhere.'

'He is very rich,' the teacher said, referring to the old man, who sat at our feet in rags. 'He has thousands of sheep and many fields of millet. He can pay for a geologist to come and find the right place for him to dig a well.'

The chief sat looking at me, not concerned or sad, but with a mischievous gleam in his eye.

'He has been waiting for many years for someone to tell him where to dig a well,' the teacher continued. The chief still sat watching me, as if at any moment I might explode.

When we came to leave the village in the late afternoon, Essmou's donkey was nowhere to be found. Search parties were sent off in all directions. One donkey was found but he was not ours. Then, just as we were resigning ourselves to a night in the village and I was nursing a secret delight at the loss of my enemy, he was brought back. Some women had caught him a long way off, attempting to steal millet from a field. He showed not the slightest hint of remorse or guilt. In fact, as usual, he looked utterly uninterested in the humans fussing around him, and only swivelled his funnel ears and frisked his tatty tail.

By this stage of our journey Essmou's confidence in me had grown and he no longer found it necessary only to speak to me in the interrogative, or to be haughty and aloof in the presence of others. We became more of a team and he could sympathise with the difficulty I was having with his donkey. When it rooted itself to the ground with me on its back, we both laughed and he said encouraging things like 'Donkeys are the most difficult of animals to ride, harder than camels or horses even.'

That evening we came across a group of women loading up a donkey

237

and preparing to go home after a day guarding a field of millet, and they asked me, 'Where is the water, where is the water?' as the village chief had done. Essmou replied, 'Don't ask him where the water is. He has not come to find your water for you. Give him some of your milk.'

They started some good-natured horseplay: the women withheld the *guerba* of milk and Essmou grabbed one of their donkeys and started to pull it away.

'Hey, give us back our donkey,' they shouted at him, and hit him playfully with small sticks. He grabbed one of them by the arm, saying he would break it unless we got the milk. Of course we got the milk in the end and the women went off singing a song about how funny it was that the white man could not find their water for them, and how strong and dangerous the Moor with him was. Or so Essmou told me.

At midday on the third day we came to a large village. On a hill of gravel in front of it was a small tin-roofed house, which we made for, and we were met at its door by a man who clasped our hands as though we were the best of friends. He was the village schoolteacher and a Moor and he invited us into his house to pass the afternoon. There was fierce wind blowing and clouds of dust followed us into the darkness of his windowless abode that rattled in its force. Inside, the house was chaotic, filled with the people and stuff of his life: trunks and sacks and tea trays and a large assortment of all that had broken and all that might be put to use. He had a mother, very old, blind and black. She sat on top of a bed with her knees drawn up to her chest, a long black robe shiny with wear falling from her head to be tucked under her toes. Her hands were long and fine and blue with veins, and as she rocked back and forth she smiled to herself. There was the teacher's young wife, a young Mooress as pretty and round as they come, and his two young children, sitting in a dark corner playing with a set of chicken's feet as if they were the most ingenious toy.

The teacher's name was Ibrahim. He was young and had a stutter

238

and a forehead wrinkled with good humour and surprise at life. He kept a flock of chickens under a bed, had some fields of millet below the hill and with these and his wages he made his life on top of the hill. He saw that Essmou and I were comfortable, fed us some milk, strangled a chicken and passed it to his wife to cook.

'What do you think I am,' he stuttered to me, 'a Harratin or a white Moor? I am neither. I am a half-caste. My father was a white Moor and my mother, as you can see, is black,' he laughed delightedly. 'But my wife, she is a white Moor, very beautiful and with a very big behind. Look, look how big it is. We like big behinds very much in Mauritania,' he explained, in an informative tone of voice. 'The bigger the better, and the more wives the better. If I were rich I would have a second wife, or even a third, then I could have many, many children, because we in Mauritania like to have many children, the more the better. Sadly, though,' he continued cheerily, 'I am not rich but very poor, because the locusts have eaten all my millet this year.'

We stayed with Ibrahim all afternoon. After we had eaten the chicken we dozed for a while, Ibrahim on the floor beside his teapot and tray, his wife beside her cooking pots, Essmou and myself on a bed, the children randomly amongst the dust and scraps, and the old mother where she sat on the bed, bowed forwards a little like a doll on a shelf. When we left Ibrahim she had not moved an inch.

We passed that night in a wide and fertile *oued*, amid the smell of moist earth and green crops and many camps and herds of livestock and carpets of fireflies that burned like city lights. Before we slept an argument broke out in one of the tents near to the one beside which we sat. Before long the argument had spread to other tents and soon it was bounding about like echoes on cliffs. When it died it was replaced by the howling of packs of dogs, snarling and fighting between their tribes and sprinting round the camps and out into the dark *oued* like demons at play.

The following day we reached Batha, at about ten o'clock in the morning and just in time for tea; a group of turbaned merchants were sitting in the shade of a house and they invited us over. Batha was just a collection of boutiques, but it had the beginnings of a town, for the Moors had come with their commerce and the people of the camps came also, to buy and sell. This was the end of our journey and where I paid Essmou for his services. There would be no transport to take me north to the Road until next day, so while Essmou passed the morning doing business and no doubt doubling his pay, I was installed on a cushion on a mattress on a mat in the shade of a lean-to in the middle of the village. There I lay, supine, and watched the day of the merchants go by. In the afternoon Essmou came to say goodbye and to tell me that he had arranged for me to stay with the young man who worked the electric mill nearby. Then he was off, mounted on a newly acquired sack of rice, merry and happy to be on his way home.

The day was extremely hot and it became increasingly hard to be sitting in the middle of the village. The boutiques closed up one by one and the merchants went off on camels and donkeys to their camps. By the time Issa, the mill worker, had closed up the mill, I was feeling quite ill from general exhaustion and too much sun. He took me to his camp – an hour's march through tall cram-cram grass that had my legs well pierced and barbed by the end – and was full of cheeriness and a thousand questions. I tried to match the spirit of my host but it was a losing battle. I was in a bad state. The world had closed in on me, my mind and vision a pounding tunnel searching for some air, some clear space. I felt oppressed and feverish and at that small and desperate stage travellers sometimes find themselves in where I just wanted to be away from all this heat and dust and difficult food and people who were all strangers. When I got to Issa's camp I said little to his friends and family, who were in a fresh, high-spirited evening mood. I bowed my roaring head and kept to myself and wondered what Issa must think of his boring and impolite guest, but he did not seem to mind. He was not a complicated young man. He was happy and content and knew that life could sometimes be hard. He left me alone and made merry with his friends all the same and next morning was glad to see me recovered.

The journey back to the Road was one of those helter-skelter rides with the driver saving minutes as though they were made of gold. We slewed along deep tracks through a land of Moors and their camels and their boutique-beginnings of towns. There were too many people and too many sheep in the back of the Landrover and an old lady was sick over me and my bag, but when once again I bumped back up on to the Road and I thought back to Mohamadu the Peul, Essmou, and Ibrahim the teacher, Issa and even the red-eyed guard, I was very glad I had stepped out in Aleg and had the opportunity to share some little bits of some other people's lives.

20

The end of the Road, Oualata and the Beduin

The people in the camel market of Nema looked gloriously unconcerned with anything but their camels and their camel- rearing life. They were vigorous and had an air of birthright independence. About their waists and their coarse tunics they wore ropes and at their hilts they carried daggers. Their proud, hawk faces spoke not of aggression but of sterner stuff than that, and their gait and pose could be matched to those of their camels, who stood pressed tight together as if at the last stand.

One man hitched up his tunic, kicked off his sandals, spat at the ground and with a single leap was on the back of a great-grandfather of a camel. The animal shot off in a fright, bellowing as he galloped, and the man, perched high on his bare back, rode him like a rodeo cowboy and soon, with the lightest touch of his heels, had the beast coursing to his will. Nearby three men suddenly threw a camel to the ground, pinning his struggling legs down and holding his long, strong neck to the earth as they branded it with a red-hot iron. Another, younger camel, having his feet inspected, struggled, broke free and charged through the market. Immediately men threw themselves at it, grabbing hold of different limbs, but the camel was strong and ploughed on, scattering other camels like birds and dropping the men off one by one. Soon there was only one man left. He was the owner and he was not going to let go. He had hold of the camel's tail and was dragged round the market like a waterskier on his bare feet. The camel bent its neck round to try to bite him but somehow the man caught hold of the ring in its nose. When he came walking calmly back with the camel on the end of a rope, the other men standing around laughed and jibed at him for the spectacle he had made.

Nema was the last town on the Road, the place where the Road came to its final and abrupt end in a heap of gravel. I was intending to slip quietly over the border south into Mali, hoping to avoid any confrontation over my various papers and permissions, which by now were hopelessly and unavoidably out of order. But before I did so I decided to do a last bit of exploration in this far corner of Mauritania, for I might never get another chance. I went north to Oualata, another of those old and dying desert caravan towns. Oualata, though, like an old warrior nearing his deathbed, was not willing to die tamely. Parts of it had indeed been abandoned and ran with sand and ruin, but much of its *medina* still rang with the sounds of true urban life. For Oualata was a piece of the Maghreb. It could have been a piece of the *medina* of Fez transported down here, for those merchants of old liked to be comfortable and sophisticated while they traded with the south. It was Maghrebian in its weave of cobbled ways and its large decorated houses, its lavish *patrons*, its hot, spicy food and its alley boys who cried, '*Guide, guide, cadeaux.*' It was urban as Chinguetti and Aoudaghost had once been and as Nouakchott was not. It still had life, just.

The *medina* grew from a hillside above a wide, empty valley; on its far side was the old French fort which now housed political prisoners, Oualata being deemed remote enough for that sort of thing. Each day the tiny ant forms of the unfortunates could be seen building a road up to the fort. Nobody in Oualata would openly admit that those ants were in fact prisoners.

At the foot of the *medina* were the buildings and barracks and the functionaries of the nation of Mauritania sent here to impose themselves upon the older order of law and power. I had dealings

244

with both sides of Oualata, the official, modern side and the older, fading one. I lodged with the adjutant of the barracks. He was a swarthy southerner and a suspicious man. He was also quiet and very despondent, because he was posted so far from his home for so long in a town where soldiers were not liked. I passed each evening with him and the family who fed him. They were not willing hosts but they were obliged to feed the adjutant and therefore the European who found himself attached to him. The evenings were intensely long and spartan and mostly silent. The father of the family, a thin, nervous man, read his Koran with, it seemed to me, an edge of desperation. Now and again he tried playing with his young son, who wailed each time he was taken from his mother. About the only subject the adjutant felt free to discuss was religion, so every now and again he and the father would break into long, heated exchanges.

I stayed with the adjutant a week and felt I did not get to know him well, but by the time I came to leave I was surprised to find that we had become friends. I don't know why, because the only things we shared were the long, boring evenings, the meagre meals and a warm 'goodnight' each time we went to bed; but friends we were and the adjutant of Oualata remains in my memory as much as anyone I met in Mauritania.

The other side of Oualata could not have been more different. Each morning the big *patrons* of the *medina*, the men of the old and rich families, would sit on walls in the alleyways conducting what was now only petty commerce, and socialising. One day, as I was walking past one of these men he called me over and invited me to his house for tea later in the day. When I went there I found it to be one of the biggest in town. It was painted with murals and rose windows and its grand, carved door was hammered in intricate ironwork of Hispanic craft like the entrance of a small palace. Inside was a cobbled courtyard with geese dabbing themselves in bowls of water, and dogs and an array of women bedecked in gold, and sons and servants of many different hues. I was directed up some steps to a large chamber where I found the *patron* lying in robed splendour on a raised dais, fondling his podgy baby daughter and talking to his wife, a veritable mammoth of a woman lounging on another dais. When I entered she got up and manoeuvred her mass to the door, collecting her bloated little daughter on the way. The *patron* had a round, humorous face that revealed a single gold tooth each time he smiled. He signalled me to take my place on the dais his wife had just vacated, and a silver bowl of yogurt and a dish of peanut cakes were produced by a servant.

The *patron* was a straightforward man and he did not mince words.

'I am very rich,' he said to me, as I admired the expensive rugs and mats that hung all over the walls, 'but do not be misled by this house. There will be people who do not eat today in this town, for this is a very poor country.' In every fibre of his lavish clothes and in his warm, round confidence he represented the older Mauritania, concerned for his country.

'Indeed,' he continued, 'some people say that we are a sad country but I say that we are not a sad country, we are a confused country. Things have been changing very fast for us since the French came here. Now we find ourselves having to adapt our ways, our morals even, to the ways and morals of an outside and far more developed world, for we are economically dependent on its aid. Some people resent this and use their religion to demonstrate this resentment. Some abuse it, as some always will, and some ignore it as for them life has not changed, it has only become a little harder because of the droughts and because the old ways of the desert have been irrevocably changed. But all feel a sense of lessening pride the more their desert dies and they are driven to the modern towns, to the main roads, to the lands of the blacks, and the more dependent they become on foreign aid.

'Do not give us money, I say to you,' the *patron* said to me as though I were an ambassador of the outside world. 'We do not want your money. Let me tell you a story. There was a fisherman who one day called his son to him. "I shall give you two choices," the fisherman said to his son. "Either I shall give you a big fish

246

to eat each day of my life or I shall teach you how to catch fish for yourself. Which do you want?" Well, the answer is obvious, is it not?' the *patron* said to me. 'By taking the first choice the son will live comfortably until his father dies. But then when his father dies he will starve because he does not know how to catch fish. By taking the second choice he will not be dependent upon his father, so will not starve when he dies. No, direct aid is the only aid we want,' the *patron* continued. 'In this town a bulldozer could do so much good, a water pump, a road even, to connect up with the modern markets of trade. Do not give us your money, it only hurts our pride and confuses the balance of power, as you can see by the state of our regime.'

One evening when I went to see the *patron* I found him in his courtyard at his prayers. Opposite him, hunkered down against a wall, was an oldish man in rags, one of the ugliest and roughest specimens of mankind I had ever seen. His face was rudely shaped and tufted with bits of beard. His nose was entirely eaten away by disease. His hair was lank and solid with dirt and grease. His hands were rough and hardened; he carried them on the ends of his arms as though they were separate, inanimate objects. His feet were so misshapen and cracked they barely merited the description, and a rich, moist smell came from his short, square body. When the *patron* had finished his devotions he told me the man was a Bedu, a herder, and that he looked after his sheep and cattle out in the brush. The Bedu, the *patron* said, was just on his way back to his camp and if I liked I could go with him. It seemed to me the *patron* wished me to go with him, as if to do so was something I should experience.

'He is nothing,' the *patron* said. 'Everything he has I own. He has and is nothing, but go with him if you wish.'

I went, and what did I find? I found what I know as poverty, poverty and hardship, at its most extreme. I found acceptance of that poverty to such a degree that I felt a huge sense of destiny, of the inevitability of it all. I found a void where there was no pride and yet no lack of pride, only survival at a most basic level. I found great simplicity and a depth of gentleness and sharing, and a beauty of smile that reminded me of the small, delicate pink flower I had once seen all on its own in the wastes of the Sahara, that had bloomed for nobody to see.

There was a long, hard walk in pitch darkness with the Bedu, a small boy, a donkey, and myself stumbling in their wake, desperate not to lose their fleeting forms. Then there was the faintest strain of light on the horizon, and then a moon and light to walk by. Then there were three tents and calls and the feeble wail of a baby. There was exhaustion and quick words, the forms of seven or eight people, mostly children, and a bowl of hot, frothy cow's milk. There was no food and there was the voice of the mother of the baby, thin and pitiful, bemoaning to her husband, the Bedu, that her baby was ill. Then the tent flaps were brought down and there was sleep, the women at one end, myself and the children and boys at the other under a single blanket. Throughout the night the baby whimpered and the mother sang quietly to it, a tiny voice in the immensity of an empty African night.

The following day there was heat, and such a heat. We passed it sitting in the tent. It did not take long to give up brushing the flies from your face or washing your hands before you ate or bothering to get up to spit from the tent the phlegm that the dusty atmosphere continually brought to your throat. Maybe it fell short on to a mat or perhaps you just wiped it on to the tent pole, too lethargic to do more than that. Throughout the day the others nibbled at the leg bone of a cow that had been lying temporarily discarded in the sand outside the tent. The Bedu picked it up and threw it on the fire before stripping it of the scraps of skin and gristle that remained. It was old and too putrid for me to eat. And there was laughter, laughter the long, terrible day through. It seemed anything, the smallest thing, would do to laugh at. While the women, who looked old and worn, sat plaiting cords of hide and nursing babies who never left their sagging breasts, and two boys sat by me studying my every possession from my camera to my socks, they laughed, laughed even when the children cried because they were ill and tired and undernourished, for everybody was undernourished and tired and a little ill; but they were as tough as the *patron*'s animals they tended and which once in a while they ate. Only and strangely, a boy or young man, as he seemed, called Bibecca was different, more vulnerable than the rest. In his face there was a Mongoloid strain that can sometimes be found in the African deserts. He was uneducated but as bright as a star and my sudden appearance had an effect upon him. In the space of a day I made perhaps my closest Mauritanian friend. He, it seemed, knew all about me and I all about him. And he, it seemed, could drop the role of the poor: to accept and not to look too far ahead. He wanted 'out' but he knew that I would not provide a way for him, so he asked of me only one thing – my socks, because he did not want his feet to be ruined like those of the older people in the camp.

I had to leave the camp that evening after only one night. One day of that heat left me feeling ill and feverish, but that was not why I left. I left because I could not cope. The bridge to here, from my home to this camp, was just too far. I could not put into perspective these people and their life. I could not stop drawing comparisons and those comparisons were too disturbing to bear. I even felt when I left that I was abandoning them, to an eternity of what to me would be hell. As if they needed me. I knew then that I had overstepped my mark. I knew my arrogance. The *patron* had known it. I shook with a kind of emotional turmoil all the long walk back to Oualata but when I got back I did not feel tired. I was filled with new enthusiasm and vigour. I was on a high. Something big had happened. Something had been given to me. I knew that. And I knew that I would be back. Not, perhaps, to the Bedu's family, not to Oualata, not even maybe to Mauritania. But I would be back. I had little choice.

...of some invisible sea. As if this...

...that I have come upon my round; I knew my wh...

...had ...e alive with a kind of ...

...to be lived ...a Quaker, but when I got back I did not feel...

I was ... ...tasy and vigour. I was on a high...

...mething had been given to me...

...perhaps, in...

William Dalrymple

In Xanadu
A Quest

In Xanadu is the story of a quest, a journey which began in the Holy Sepulchre of Jerusalem and took William Dalrymple and his companions across Asia in the steps of Marco Polo to the dais of Kubla Khan's throne, the seat of Coleridge's celebrated Xanadu itself.

'Absolutely glorious.'   *Patrick Leigh Fermor*

'All manner of echoes: Freya Stark, Peter Fleming, Robert Byron . . . Dalrymple is plainly either brilliant, or bonkers, or both.'   Alan Franks, *The Times*

'A glorious and involving read in the best Newby and Raban traditions.'   Frank Delaney

flamingo

Carolyn Cassady

Off the Road

Twenty Years with Cassady, Kerouac and Ginsberg

Carolyn Cassady's account of life off the road with her husband Neal Cassady, her lover Jack Kerouac and the lover of both, Allen Ginsberg, exerts a powerful fascination. Monster, madman, saint and delinquent, Neal Cassady lived what others could only dream: Kerouac's immortalisation of him as the hero of *On the Road*, Dean Moriarty, launched a new era in literature.

'Carolyn Cassady's book is the one that I have been waiting to read for the past forty years, the one that sets the record straight for the first time . . . This is a book about the end of innocence in America. It's one hell of a story.'   Jay Landesman, *Sunday Times*

'This is the book to read in tandem with Kerouac's *On the Road*. Ginsberg's *Howl* and Tom Wolfe's *Electric Kool Aid Acid Test*. It fits like the lost half of a broken plate.'   *Literary Review*

'An intensely readable account.'   Peter Ackroyd, *The Times*

'*Off the Road* is a touching intimate memoir that offers a nakedly frank account of events. This might just turn out to be *the* Beat memoir.'   *Blitz*

flamingo

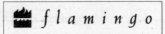

flamingo

Flamingo is a quality imprint publishing both fiction and non-fiction. Below are some recent titles.

Fiction

☐ The Things They Carried *Tim O'Brien* £4.99
☐ Matilda's Mistake *Anne Oakley* £4.99
☐ Acts of Worship *Yukio Mishima* £4.99
☐ My Cousin, My Gastroenterologist *Mark Leyner* £4.99
☐ Escapes *Joy Williams* £4.99
☐ The Dust Roads of Monferrato *Rosetta Loy* £4.99
☐ The Last Trump of Avram Blok *Simon Louvish* £4.99
☐ Captain Vinegar's Commission *Philip Glazebrook* £4.99
☐ Gate at the End of the World *Philip Glazebrook* £4.99
☐ Ordinary Love *Jane Smiley* £4.99

Non-fiction

☐ A Stranger in Tibet *Scott Berry* £4.99
☐ The Quantum Self *Danah Zohar* £4.99
☐ Ford Madox Ford *Alan Judd* £6.99
☐ C. S. Lewis *A. N. Wilson* £5.99
☐ Meatless Days *Sara Suleri* £4.99
☐ Finding Connections *P. J. Kavanagh* £4.99
☐ Shadows Round the Moon *Roy Heath* £4.99
☐ Sweet Summer *Bebe Moore Campbell* £4.99

You can buy Flamingo paperbacks at your local bookshop or newsagent. Or you can order them from Fontana Paperbacks, Cash Sales Department, Box 29, Douglas, Isle of Man. Please send a cheque, postal or money order (not currency) worth the purchase price plus 22p per book (or plus 22p per book if outside the UK).

NAME (Block letters)_____

ADDRESS_____

_____

_____